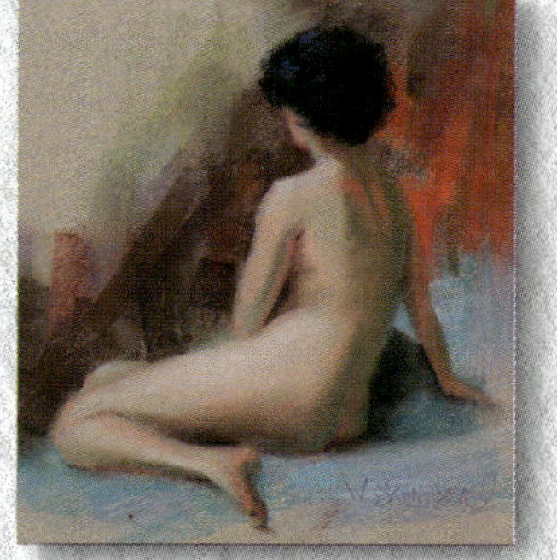

Pastel 2

Pastel is a fascinating and versatile medium that is a joy to work with. The colors can be rich and vibrant or soft and subdued, and you can create many interesting and varied textures. There are no colors to mix or thinners to use, and the fact that it's dry makes it a wonderful medium for traveling and painting outdoors. Most important, pastel allows for a variety of blending and layering techniques that are virtually impossible with any other medium. In this book, I'll share my methods for painting a number of pastel subjects—from the initial sketches to the finishing touches. And I'll explain my approach and techniques with simple, step-by-step lessons to give you a new appreciation of this wonderful art form. I hope you will be inspired to explore the many creative possibilities that pastel has to offer! —*William Schneider*

CONTENTS

Selecting Pastel Supplies ... 2

Introducing Color Theory ... 4

Exploring Basic Techniques ... 6

Planning a Composition ... 8

Creating Depth ... 10

Expressing Mood ... 12

Rendering Light with Value ... 14

Portraying Animals ... 16

Capturing a Likeness ... 18

Using Colored Paper ... 20

Developing the Human Form ... 22

Depicting Flowers ... 24

Detecting Color in White ... 26

Deciding What to Paint ... 28

Painting Outdoors ... 30

Walter Foster Art Instruction Program ... 32

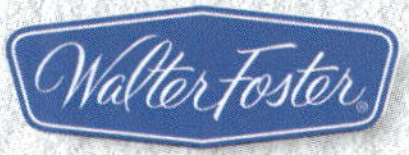

Selecting Pastel Supplies

Yand you don't need many supplies to begin painting in pastel; unlike oil or acrylic paints, pastels don't require additives or brushes. All you really need to get started is a set of pastels and a variety of papers (or *supports*). Then just add a few additional tools and materials described on these pages, and you'll be ready to paint in pastel!

PURCHASING SOFT PASTELS

Pastels are available in several forms—including oil pastels and hard, clay-based pastel sticks and pastel pencils—but I work with soft pastels. These chalklike sticks are a popular choice, as they produce a beautiful, velvety texture and are easy to blend with your fingers or a cloth. When purchasing pastels, keep in mind that pastel colors are mixed on the paper as you paint, rather than premixed on a palette. (See page 5.) Therefore I suggest that you buy a wide range of colors in various *values*—lights, mediums, and darks—so you will always have the color you want readily at hand.

APPLYING FIXATIVE

Because soft pastels have less binder than hard pastels, they crumble easily, and your finished work can be smudged. So many artists use some type of spray-on sealer or fixative to set their work and prevent it from smearing. (See the demonstration at right.) I don't fix my paintings because I don't like the way the varnish affects the quality of the pastel. Instead I prefer to preserve my artwork by keeping the layers of pastel very thin as I create the painting. Then when I'm finished, I tap the support several times so that the excess pigment falls off. Then I have my painting double-matted and framed under UV light-protected glass. A pastel painting that's properly mounted on archival paper will last for centuries.

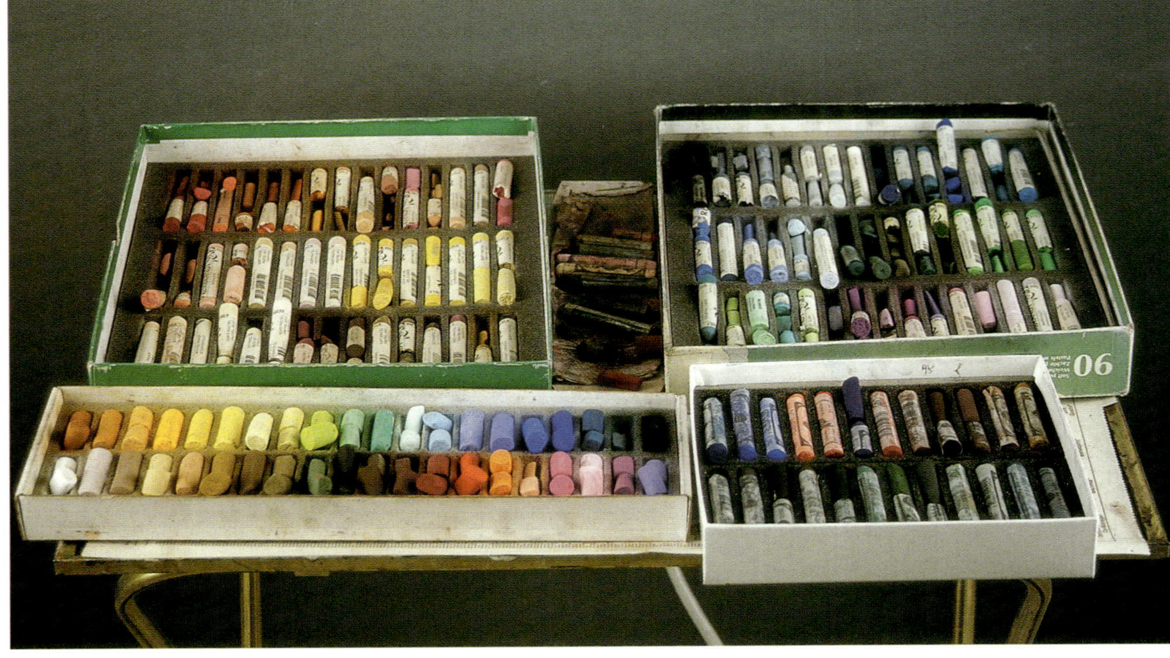

PICKING SOFT PASTELS My basic set (shown above) consists of an assortment of 90 medium soft pastels, another assortment of 40 very soft half-sticks, and a set of 24 deep darks. If you've never worked in soft pastel, I recommend that you buy a 45- or 60-stick set created specifically for beginners. If you have a choice, look for a set that has a wide range of reds, blues, and yellows. But if you prefer to buy individual colors, I suggest starting with black, white, and four values—3, 5, 7, and 9—of permanent red, ultramarine blue deep, and cadmium yellow light (See page 5 for a description of the numbering system.) You can create additional tones by layering and blending these basics, and you can always add more colors later as you develop your own style and preferred palette of colors.

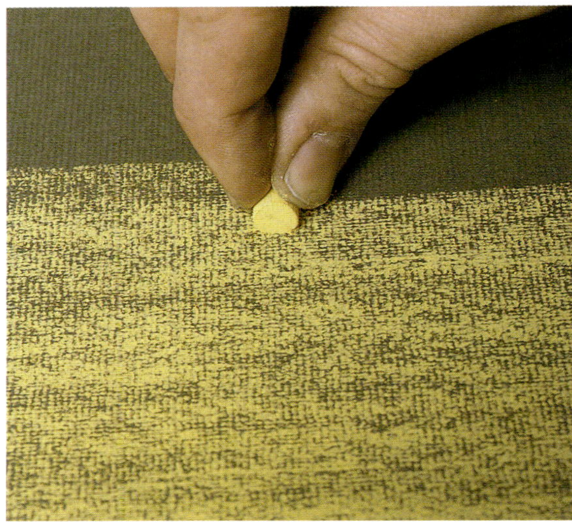

FIXING STAGE ONE To decide whether the fixative you have will adversely affect the colors, make a practice test by laying down a thick layer of pigment on a piece of pastel paper.

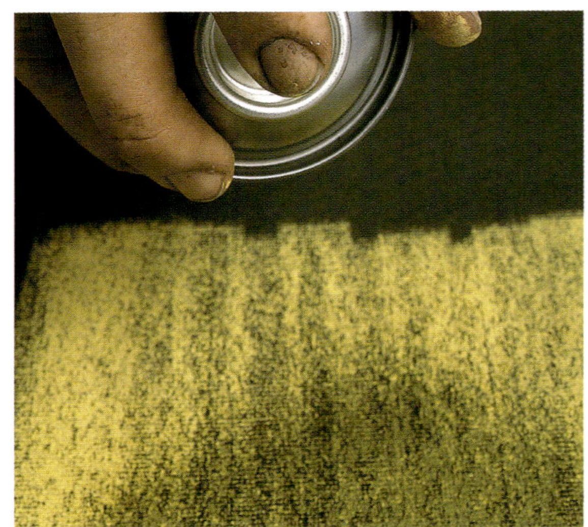

FIXING STAGE TWO Spray the piece with an even layer of fixative. If the color stays true, you can varnish your work as you go, painting over each fixed layer without the risk of smudging.

▶ GATHERING EXTRAS In addition to pastels, a few other tools will help you as you paint. I use scissors to trim my supports and vine charcoal to lay out my designs. (Vine charcoal is easy to erase and can be painted over with pastel.) I also use a sandpaper block as a sharpener, a paper stump for blending, and a razor blade to break the pastels cleanly. And sometimes I paint over my work with denatured alcohol on a soft brush to wash the color thoroughly into the paper.

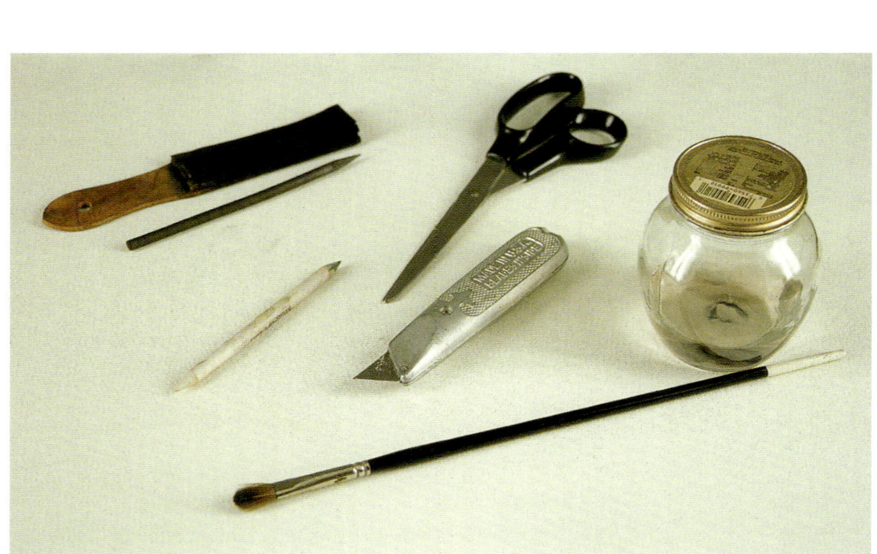

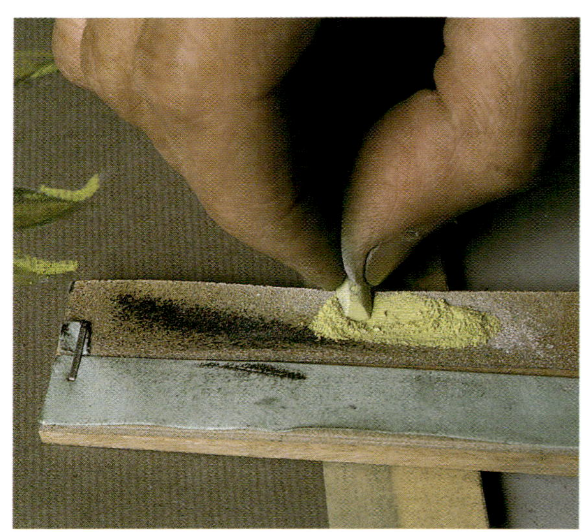

SHARPENING PASTELS A sandpaper block is a good sharpening tool for both charcoal and pastel. You can also hone pastels with a razor blade, but rubbing the stick gently across sandpaper or another rough-grained surface is a safer way to form a point or chiseled edge.

CHOOSING SUPPORTS

The texture and color of the support you choose will affect your pastel painting. Because of the delicate nature of soft pastels, you need a paper that has some *tooth*, or grain, for the pigment to stick to. A rough support, such as sanded paper (made especially for pastel application), will "break up" the applied strokes and create texture, while a smooth surface, such as pastel or watercolor paper, will make the unbroken colors appear more intense. Pastel supports are also available in a variety of colors; you can choose a color that offers a contrasting background tone or one that is in the same color range as your subject. (For more on using colored supports, see the examples below right and the text on page 20.)

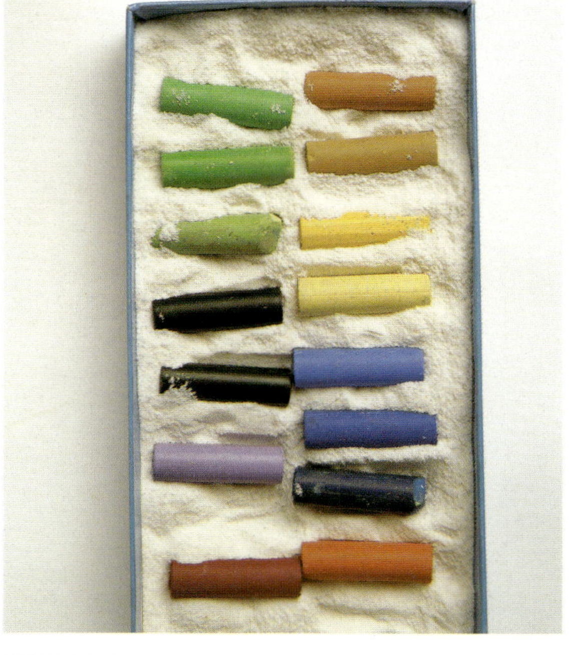

USING TEXTURED GROUNDS Rough papers are perfect for creating textured effects—the rougher the paper, the more it will break up the color. Rough-grained supports can also help convey the look of foliage, stucco, or fur.

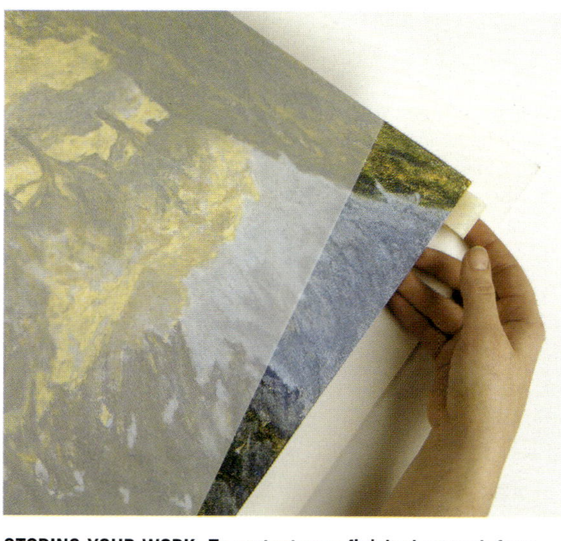

PAINTING ON SMOOTH PAPER Smoother papers are wonderful choices for rendering detailed work and soft blends. Keep in mind that the smooth side of pastel paper actually holds more pigment than the rough side.

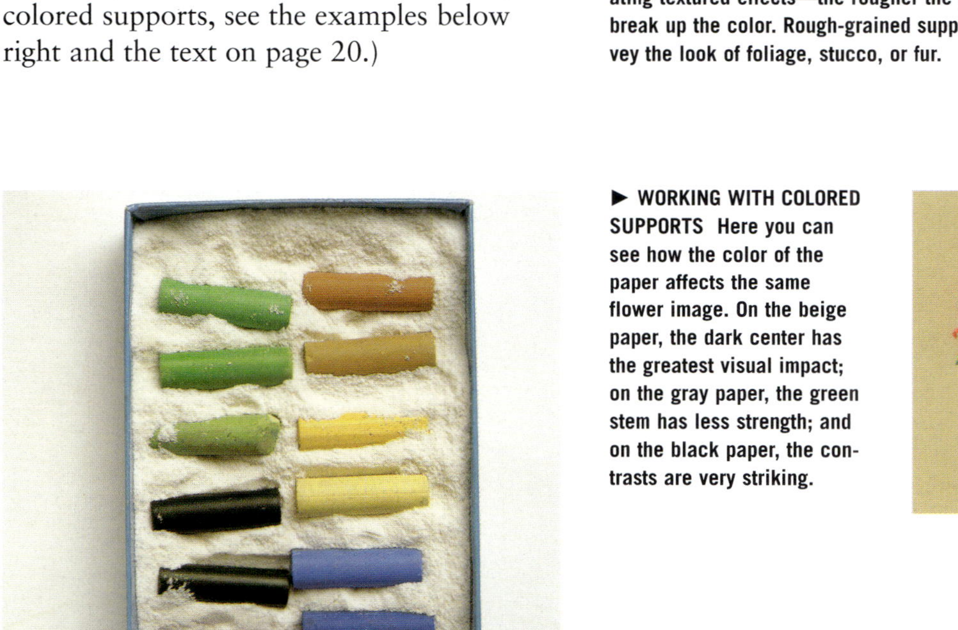

► WORKING WITH COLORED SUPPORTS Here you can see how the color of the paper affects the same flower image. On the beige paper, the dark center has the greatest visual impact; on the gray paper, the green stem has less strength; and on the black paper, the contrasts are very striking.

KEEPING PASTELS CLEAN The powdery texture of pastels can make them messy to handle and store, but you can avoid this problem by storing your soft pastels in raw rice.

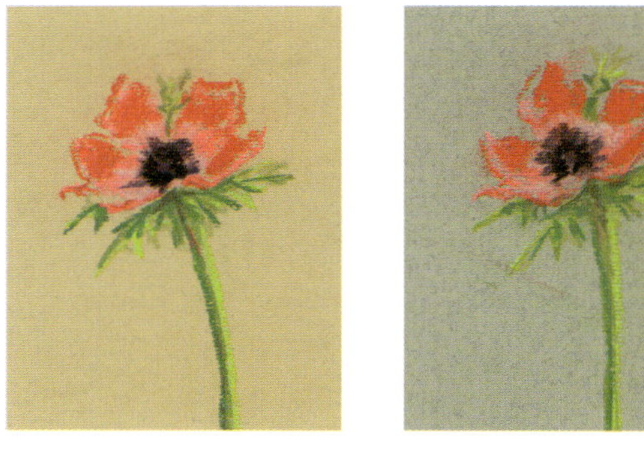

STORING YOUR WORK To protect your finished artwork from smudging or smearing, always store your pastel paintings between a board and a cover sheet. You can purchase artist's tissue paper by the roll and cut it to fit your painting; then affix the paper to the back of the support with low-tack artist's tape.

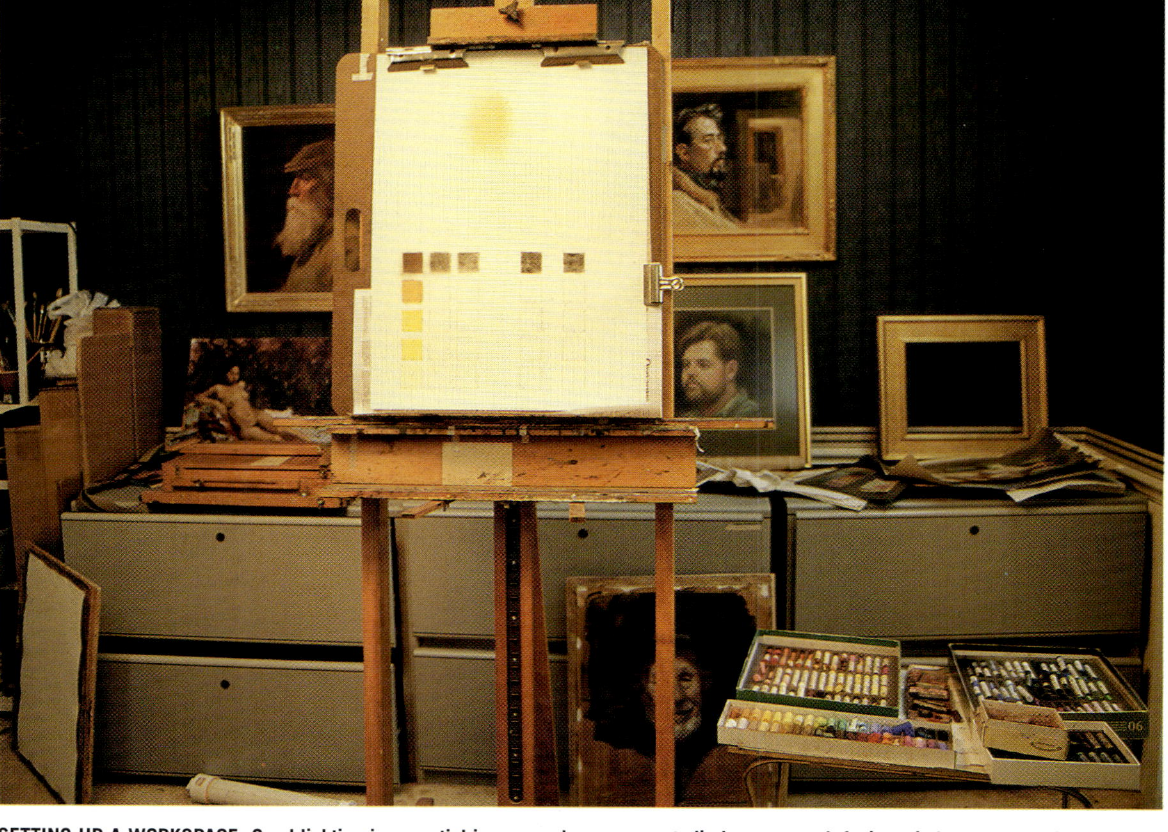

SETTING UP A WORKSPACE Good lighting is essential in any workspace; my studio has two north-facing windows that provide constant, cool light. Directly above each window, I have a large fluorescent floor-lamp with color-corrected bulbs. I work on a large, studio easel on rollers that can easily be moved. I also built an 18"-high platform (on rollers) for my models, so that when they pose for me, I can stand while I paint and still have my subject at eye level. I keep my pastels in their original boxes, sorted by color and value, on an old TV table to the right of my easel. I always return each pastel to its original slot when I'm done with it, so I don't have hunt for it again while I'm painting—or pick up the wrong one by mistake! I also keep a large mirror mounted on another easel nearby. As I paint, I frequently look at my painting in the mirror; the reflection offers another viewpoint to check for inaccuracies in my work.

Introducing Color Theory

You may already know something about color theory, but here are a few basic terms and concepts I'll refer to in this book. The *primary* colors (traditionally red, yellow, and blue) are the three basic colors that can't be created by mixing other colors; all other colors are derived from these three. *Secondary* colors are each a combination of two primary colors, and *tertiary* colors are a combination of a primary color and a secondary color. *Complementary* colors are any two directly across from each other on the color wheel, as shown at right, and the term *hue* refers to the color itself.

USING THE MUNSELL COLOR SYSTEM

I follow the Munsell Color System, which is a variation on the system based on the traditional color wheel. In the Munsell system, purple and green are also treated as primary colors, which shifts the placement of blue and yellow on the color wheel (below right). This in turn creates different complementary colors. For example, on the traditional wheel, the complement of red is green; in the Munsell system, the complement of red is blue-green. The difference between the two systems is subtle but important; when you mix complements in the traditional system, you don't get true neutral grays—for example, red mixed with green produces a warm, brownish gray. But if you mix red and blue-green, you get a truer, more neutral gray.

UNDERSTANDING COLOR "TEMPERATURE"

We often refer to colors in terms of temperature, meaning they convey a sense of warmth or coolness. In general, reds, yellow, and oranges are considered warm, and blues, greens, and purples are thought of as cool. But there are also cool and warm variations of every hue; for example, a red with more yellow in it would be a warm red, and a red with more blue in it would be a cool red. Consequently your painting will impart an overall feeling of warmth or coolness depending on which colors dominate.

THE STANDARD COLOR WHEEL In this color wheel, the traditional primary colors of red, yellow, and blue are shown on the outer ring. The inner ring illustrates the traditional secondary colors; orange, green, and purple. In this system, you can see that the complementary colors are red and green, yellow and purple, and blue and orange.

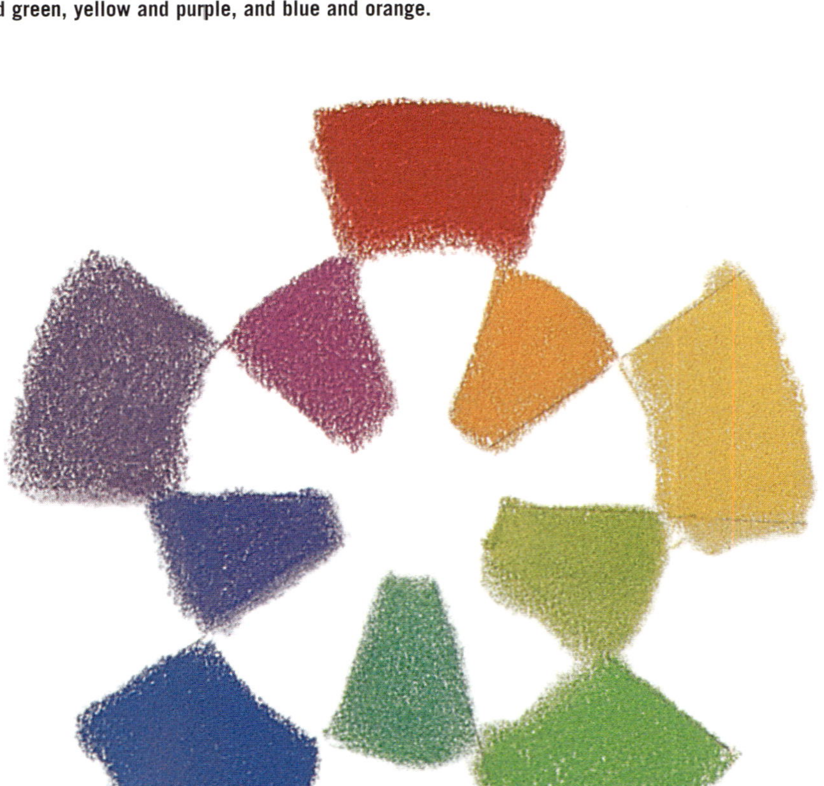

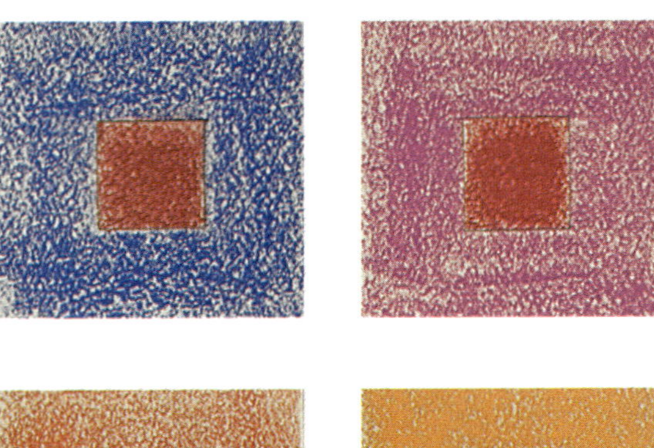
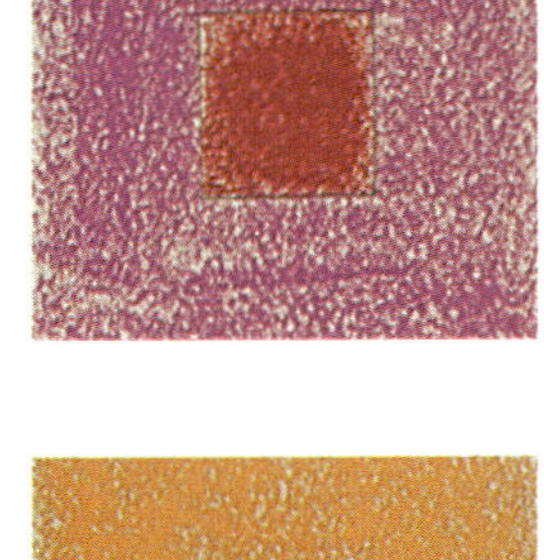
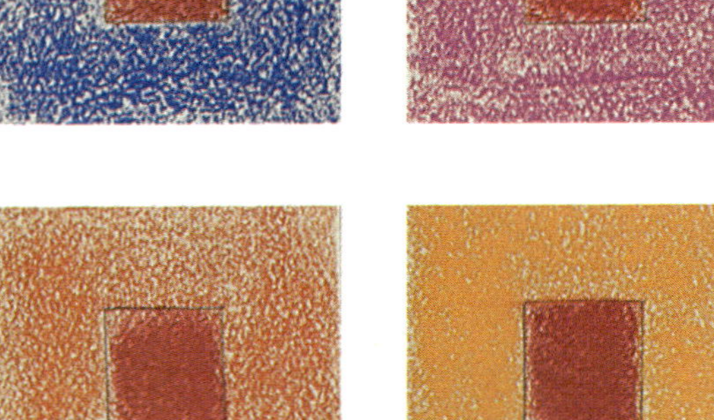

▶ APPLYING THE CONCEPT OF COLOR "TEMPERATURE" In practice, colors are perceived of as warm or cool only in relation to one another. Here I've painted a square of the same red on different backgrounds. Next to a cool blue, the red appears warm. Against red-violet, it also appears warm, but with much less temperature contrast. When placed on red-orange, the red seems cooler, and next to a warm orange background it appears quite cool. When painting, always view each area in terms of the temperature of the colors around it.

THE MUNSELL COLOR WHEEL On the Munsell color wheel, the primary colors are also on the outer ring and the secondaries are again in the inner ring. But with green and purple as additional primaries, the complementary pairs in this system are red and blue-green, yellow and blue-purple, green and red-purple, blue and orange, and purple and yellow-green.

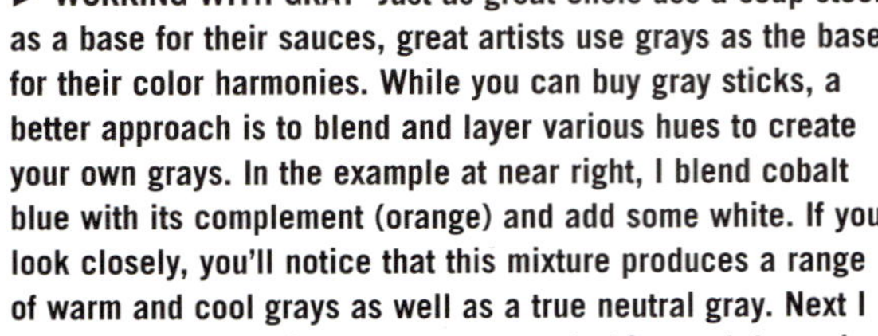

▶ WORKING WITH GRAY Just as great chefs use a soup stock as a base for their sauces, great artists use grays as the base for their color harmonies. While you can buy gray sticks, a better approach is to blend and layer various hues to create your own grays. In the example at near right, I blend cobalt blue with its complement (orange) and add some white. If you look closely, you'll notice that this mixture produces a range of warm and cool grays as well as a true neutral gray. Next I blend cobalt blue with yellow-green and white, and then mix cobalt blue with red-purple and white. Note that although these other two mixtures don't result in the creation of true grays, they do create a range of neutral gray tones.

UNDERSTANDING VALUE

Pastel manufacturers produce each hue in a variety of full-strength colors. They also make a wide range of dark and light values by adding black (creating a *shade*) or white (creating a *tint)* to the pure color. And most manufacturers label their pastels using a numbering system to identify the strength of each color. Unfortunately these numbering systems are not standardized among brands. With the pastels I use, a value of 5 indicates the pure color. A value of 3 or 1 indicates a darker value of the hue, and a value of 7 or 8 indicates that some white has been added to the pure pigment to create a lighter value. The higher the number above 5, the lighter the value. A value of 12 is almost completely white. When you purchase pastels, it's a good idea to create a labeled chart like the one at right to help you identify the various pastels you have at your disposal.

MIXING COLORS

Although it is more convenient to have a wide range of colors and values in your pastel set, you can mix additional colors directly on your support by layering and blending your soft pastels. The chart at the bottom of the page demonstrates various ways you can mix colors on your paper. You can blend the strokes thoroughly to create a solid area of smooth color, or you can leave visible strokes of various hues if you want more texture.

PURCHASING A VARIETY OF VALUES You can buy just about any value you'd want, so it's easy to get carried away and purchase half a dozen variations of the same hue. However, you can keep your expense to a minimum by starting out with just 4 basic values. This chart shows four different values of four different colors. To substitute for the values you don't have, you can always blend in a little white to create a lighter value (creating a tint) or a touch of black (creating a shade) to give yourself more options.

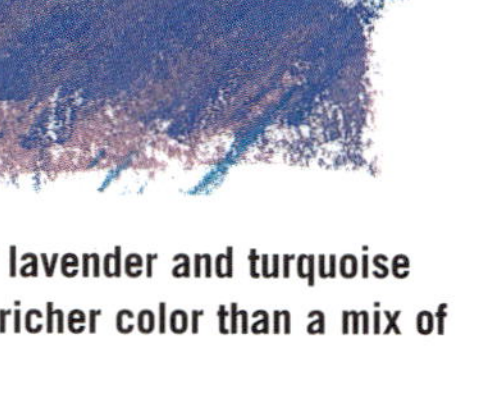

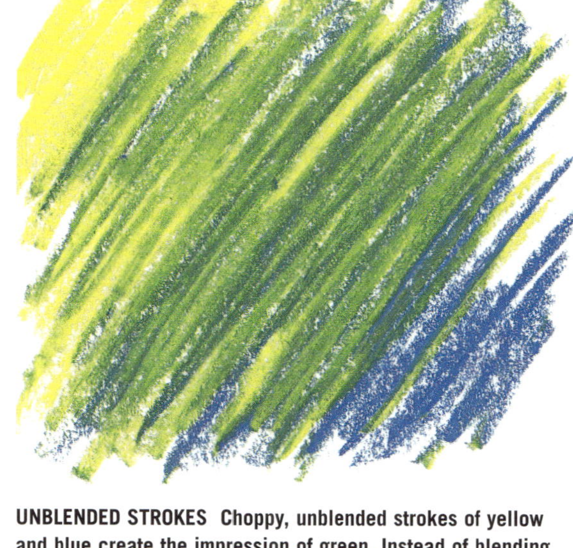

SMOOTH BLEND Here side strokes of yellow are layered smoothly over blue to create a bright green, which has more life and interest than a manufactured green.

UNBLENDED STROKES Choppy, unblended strokes of yellow and blue create the impression of green. Instead of blending the colors on the paper, the eye visually mixes them.

THREE COLOR MIXES Here strokes of lavender and turquoise are layered over blue. This creates a richer color than a mix of just two colors does.

Exploring Basic Techniques

What makes soft pastel such a fascinating medium is that it is somewhere between drawing and painting—you use pastel strokes and lines to render a subject as you would in a drawing, but the thick, buttery consistency of the medium allows you to cover the support almost the way you do with paint. But unlike painting with a brush or drawing with a pencil, painting with pastels allows you immediate contact with the support—you can apply color without the use of any tools. This means that the amount of blending you do, the type of stroke you use, and the pressure you apply will all directly affect the art you create. Once you learn some of the basic techniques presented here, you will be able to decide which you are most comfortable with and which will give you the results you desire.

BLENDING SOFT PASTELS

When you are covering an area with a solid color (whether a single hue or a mix of two or more), you can either leave the strokes visible for added texture or blend them for a smooth application of color; blending will produce a more painterly effect. I like to blend my initial applications of color and then place bolder unblended strokes nearby to create a dramatic contrast. Although I sometimes use a blending tool or paper towel to blend my pastels, I generally use my hands and fingers. They're much more immediate, and I have more control over the outcome when I can actually feel the pigment beneath my hands. (Just be sure to wipe your fingers after each stroke to keep your colors clean.)

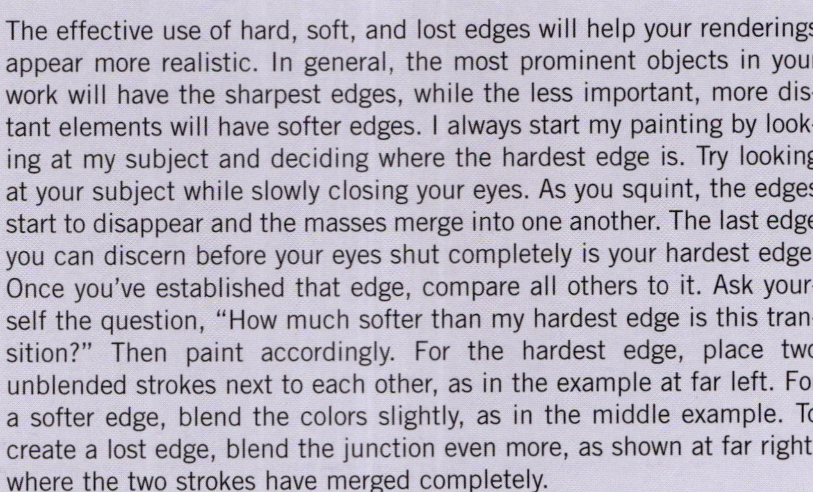

BLENDING WITH MY HAND For large smooth areas like water and skies (or even skin), I use the side of my hand and work the pastel deeply into the tooth of the paper. This ensures that no "pock marks" in the paper will appear and break up the form.

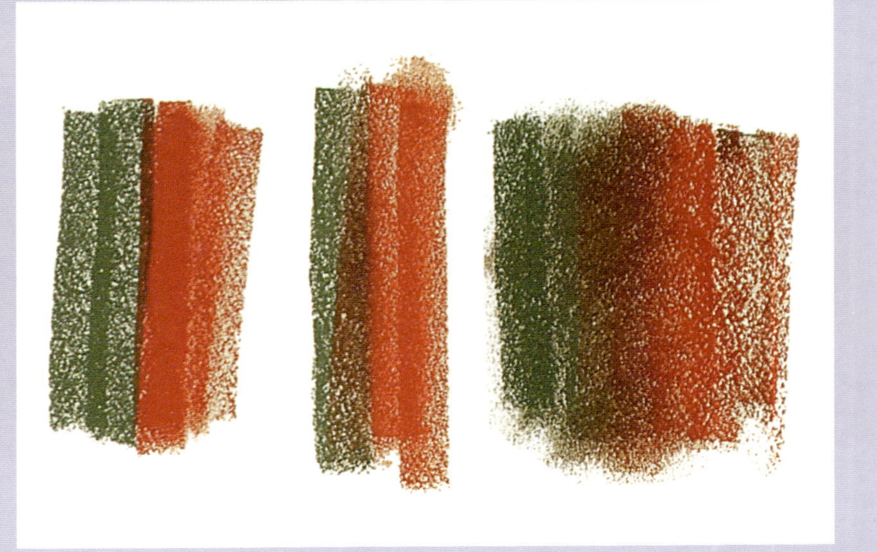

BLENDING WITH MY FINGER For a subtle blend in a small area, I often use the tip of my little finger to smudge the pigment. Blending the pastel strokes creates a smooth appearance for objects with little texture, like metal, glass, or skin.

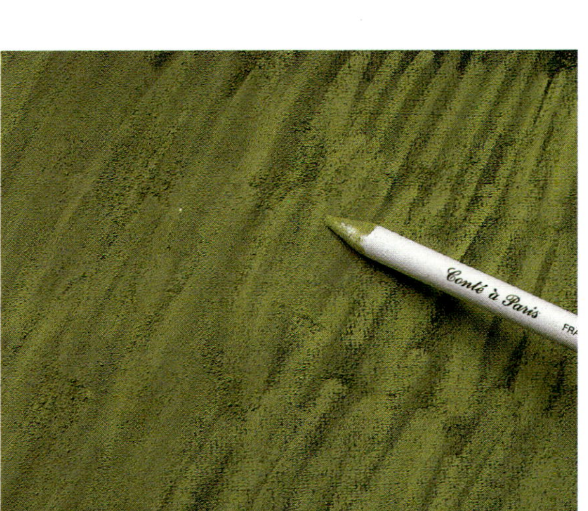

BLENDING WITH A TORTILLON For soft blends in smaller areas where my finger won't fit, I gently rub a *tortillon,* or paper blending stump, over the pigment. This works well for smooth surfaces like distant grass or fog.

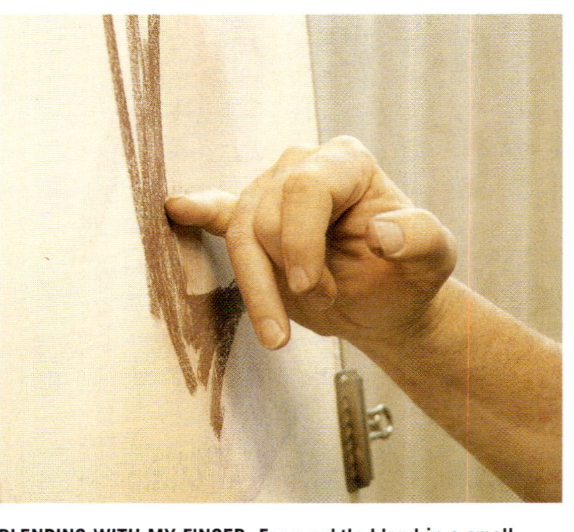

USING A CLOTH For a large background, I sometimes use a cloth or paper towel to blend the colors. Or to lighten an area, I remove the powdery excess pastel by wiping it off with a soft paper towel.

Painting Edges

The effective use of hard, soft, and lost edges will help your renderings appear more realistic. In general, the most prominent objects in your work will have the sharpest edges, while the less important, more distant elements will have softer edges. I always start my painting by looking at my subject and deciding where the hardest edge is. Try looking at your subject while slowly closing your eyes. As you squint, the edges start to disappear and the masses merge into one another. The last edge you can discern before your eyes shut completely is your hardest edge. Once you've established that edge, compare all others to it. Ask yourself the question, "How much softer than my hardest edge is this transition?" Then paint accordingly. For the hardest edge, place two unblended strokes next to each other, as in the example at far left. For a softer edge, blend the colors slightly, as in the middle example. To create a lost edge, blend the junction even more, as shown at far right, where the two strokes have merged completely.

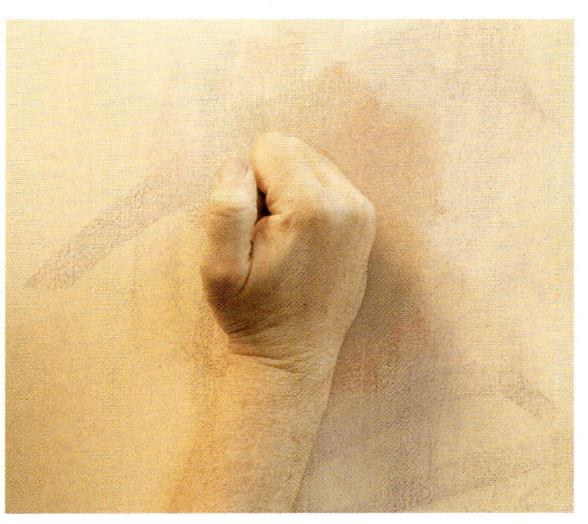

EXPERIMENTING WITH DIFFERENT STROKES

Pastel can be applied with linear strokes (more like a drawing than a painting) and either be left alone or blended in a variety of ways. You can also create a variety of textures and special effects by using the point or side of a pastel or manipulating the color with a brush or blending stump. Here are some examples of linear strokes you can practice and a few special techniques you can try out as you explore different methods of working with pastel.

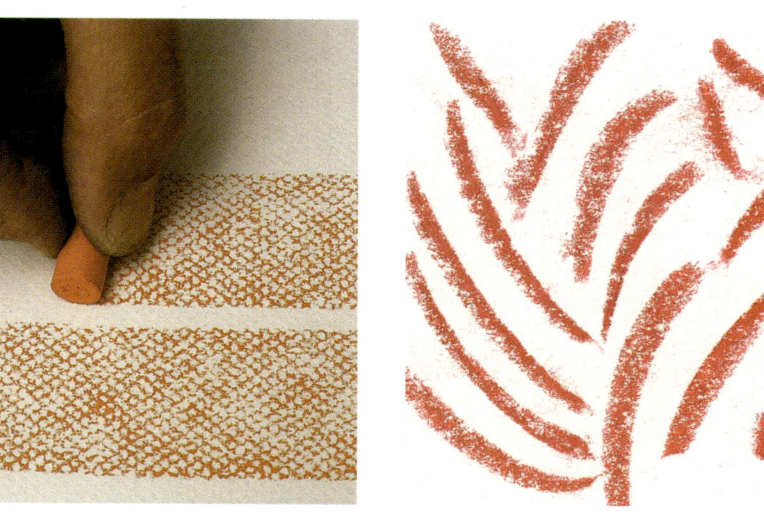

SIDE STROKES Use the entire length of the pastel stick to quickly cover the support and fill in areas of broad color, as for skies and ground cover.

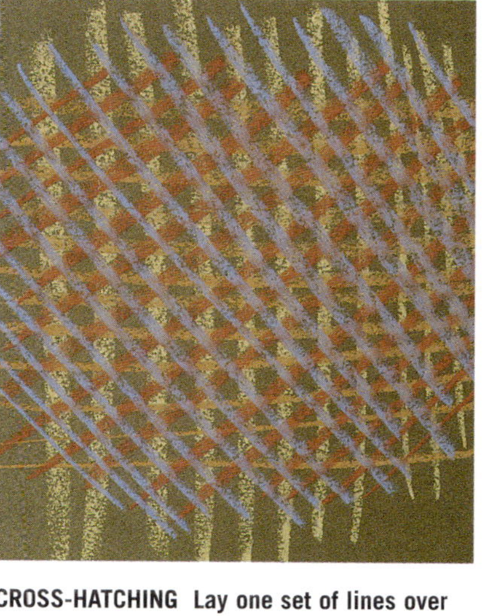

FIRM STROKES Use heavy pressure and the tip of the pastel stick to create thick, bold strokes for linear elements like stems and branches.

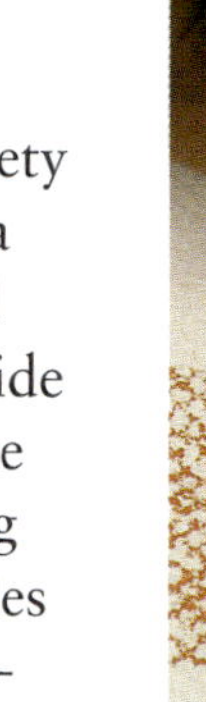

TAPERED STROKES Apply more pressure at the bottom of the stroke, and lighten the pressure as you stroke up to create grasses and leaves or fur and feathers.

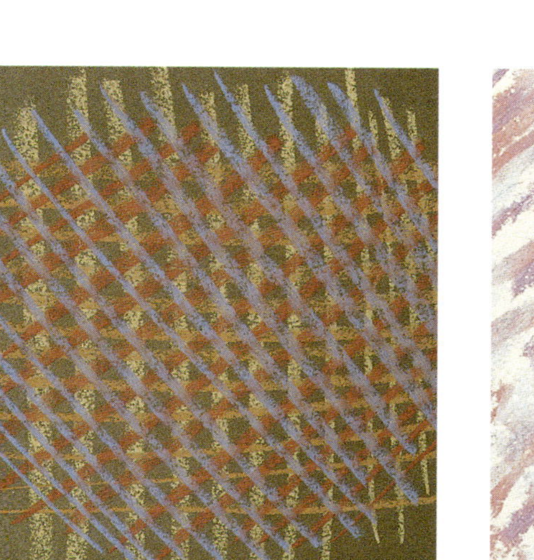

VARYING THE PRESSURE Use heavier pressure (at top) to make thick, dark lines for still water, and lighter pressure (at bottom) for the thinner, broken strokes for waves and ripples.

CROSS-HATCHING Lay one set of lines over another (in a different direction) for cross-hatching to imitate a pattern or depict the texture in cloth.

FEATHERING Layer feathery, light, diagonal strokes of various colors to create the rough texture of stucco or rock, the uneven ground, or a swift-moving river.

WET LINES Use a soft brush dipped in clean water to paint over strokes of pastel to create contrasting hard and soft edges in foliage and bark.

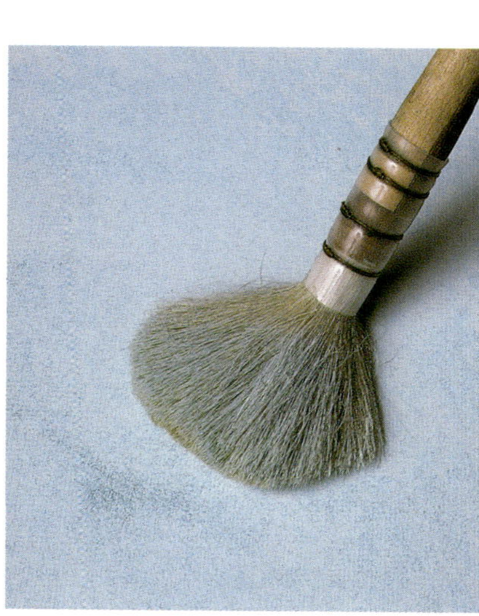

GRADATIONS Blend with a paper stump or layer colors over one another to create a multi-hued gradation for a sunset or sunrise.

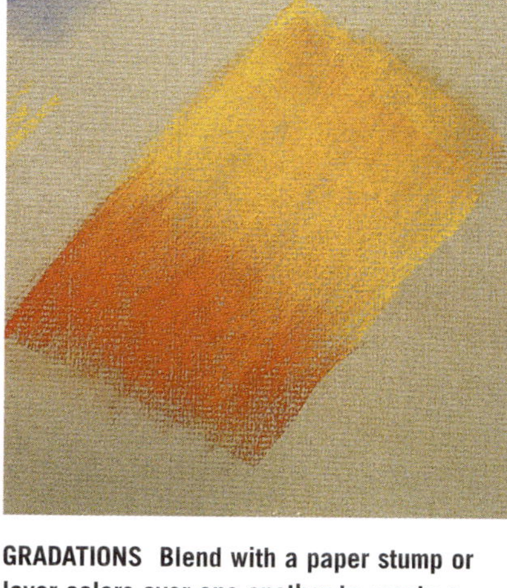

TONING THE SUPPORT Use a soft blending brush to even out an application of color, creating a smooth base for a sky.

SCUMBLING Although *scumbling* is traditionally an oil painting technique for lightly layering dry colors, you can scumble with pastel by layering light, circular strokes of color over one another. This loose blend can help to create the appearance of texture for such things as sand or water.

Planning a Composition

A successful painting has more than just an appealing subject; it also has an appealing composition. *Composition* refers to the way objects are placed in a painting and how they relate to one another. The elements in a good composition are grouped into a balanced unit, and there is a distinct center of interest, or *focal point*. A strong composition comprises interesting colors, shapes, and lines, which lead the viewer's eye through the painting and toward the focal point. Here I arranged the onions to create a visual path toward the white carafe, which is placed off-center to guide the eye through the painting. The onion peel on the far left counterbalances the forms on the right, whereas the peel on the far right acts as a "stopper," preventing the eye from wandering off the paper and keeping the focus on the onions and carafe.

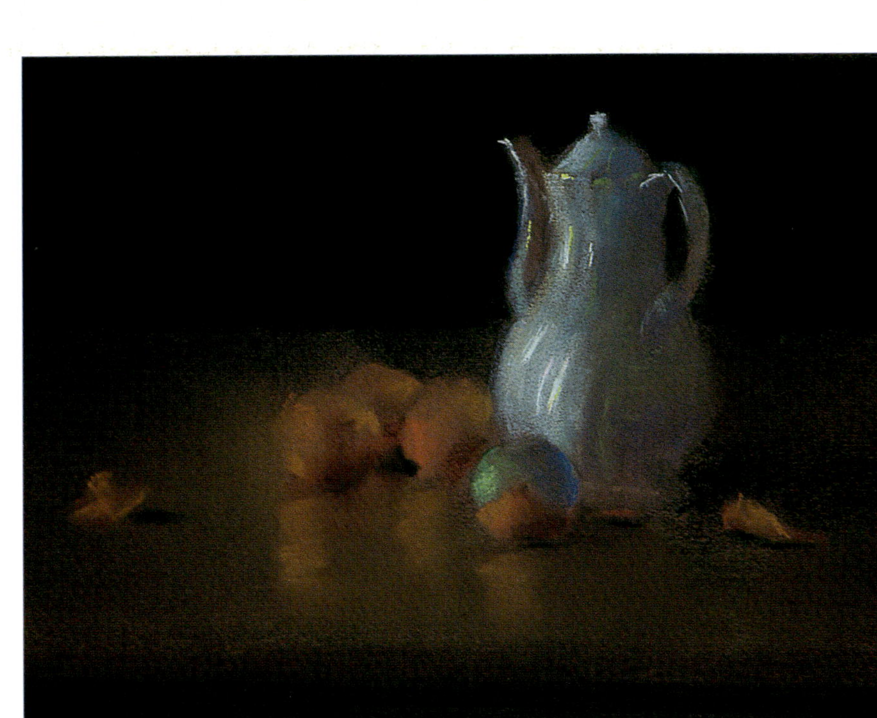

1 The dominant tone is dark, so I begin by painting the background with layers of black, carmine brown 2 (meaning a value of 2), and purple 3, blending well with my hand. I paint the table with burnt sienna 3 and yellow ochre 3, working these colors into the tooth of the paper with the side of my hand. I let some of the black background blend into the table on the far left. Then I apply a strip of black and carmine brown 2 to indicate the space beneath the tabletop. These warm darks will offset the cool light illuminating this still life.

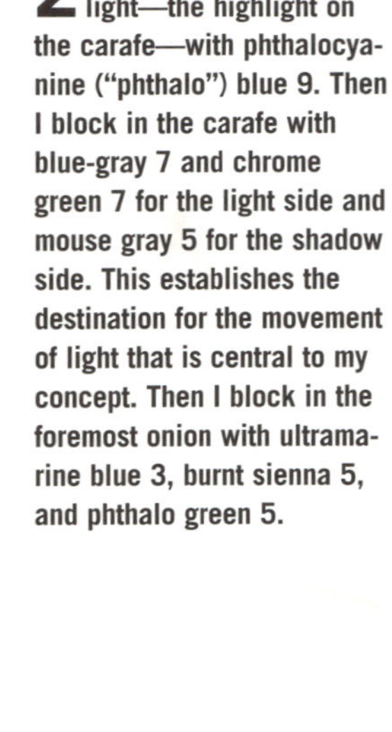

▲ STARTING WITH A DRAWING For this painting, I start by placing the center of interest about a third of the way from the right. Using a centerline to keep my drawing straight, I sketch the shape of the carafe with vine charcoal. Then I outline the onions and peels. At this stage, I draw the onions as a single mass—I'll separate them later as I paint.

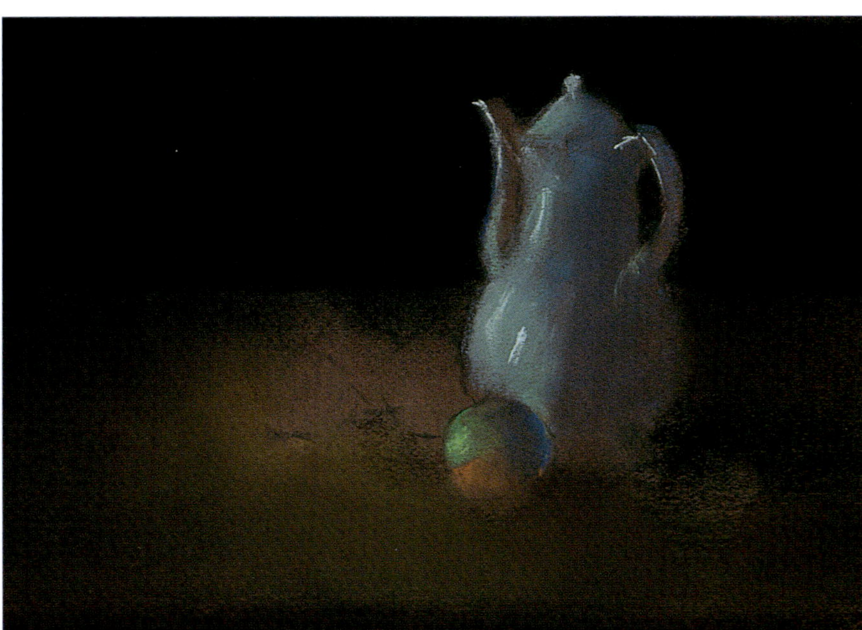

2 Next I paint the lightest light—the highlight on the carafe—with phthalocyanine ("phthalo") blue 9. Then I block in the carafe with blue-gray 7 and chrome green 7 for the light side and mouse gray 5 for the shadow side. This establishes the destination for the movement of light that is central to my concept. Then I block in the foremost onion with ultramarine blue 3, burnt sienna 5, and phthalo green 5.

CONVEYING A CONCEPT

Although beginning artists often believe the intent of a painting is to depict objects as accurately as possible, more advanced artists use objects to convey an abstract idea or concept. The objects in this still life are not as important to me as what the composition itself communicates to my viewer; I could easily use apples or oranges in place of the onions. What matters to me is creating the sense movement of light from left to right, so I deliberately make the nonessential elements—the table and background—extremely dark. I also place the onions so they lead the eye to the center of interest. This way the onions are brighter the closer they are to the light, naturally drawing the eye in the same direction and effectively illustrating my original concept.

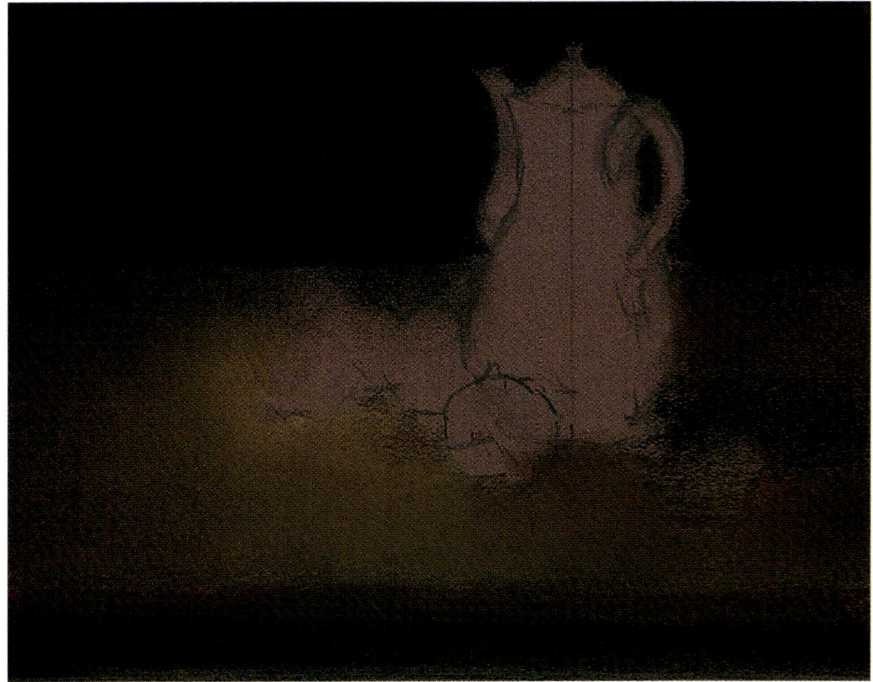

3 Now I block in the rest of the onions. I use raw umber 3 and carmine 3 for the shadow sides and raw sienna 3 and 5 for the light sides. I anchor the onions to the tabletop with accents of carmine brown 2, and I use brown ochre 3 for the reflections. Then I draw in the shapes of the peels with raw sienna 3. At this point, I blend all my strokes with the side of my finger to keep my rendering soft.

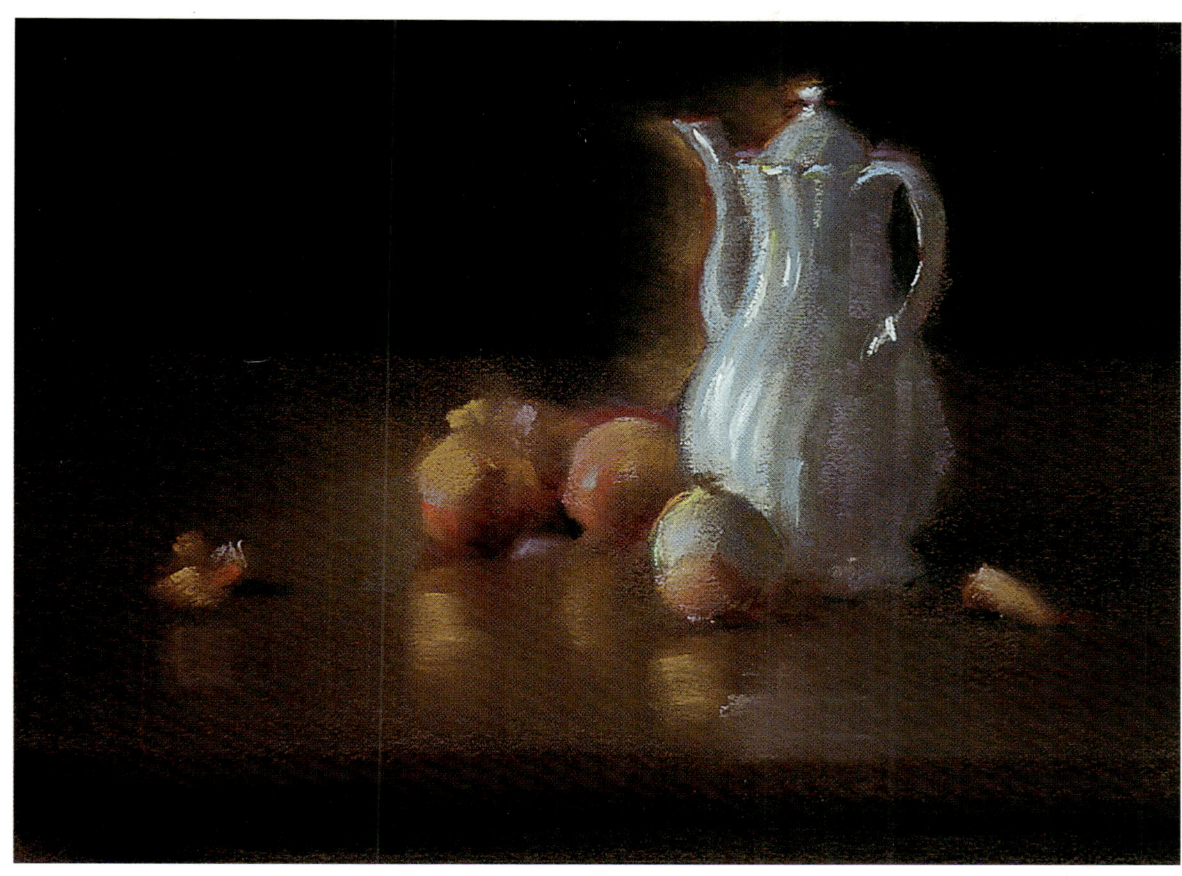

4 Next I blend vermilion 5, orange 3, and purple 5 into the area around the carafe and add some permanent red dark 5 above the onion closest to the carafe. Then I lighten the carafe with chrome green 9 and sharpen the highlights with white. I lighten the other three onions and their reflections with gold ochre 5 and phthalo green 5, and I stroke in some light behind the left onion with violet 5. Next I paint the stem on the foremost onion with madder brown 3 and then add highlights on the other onions with red-violet 5 and phthalo green 9. Always thinking about my concept, I'm careful to keep the onion on the left darker than the onion closest to the carafe. I cool the "halo" around the carafe with blue-violet 5 and ultramarine blue 5, and I use black and carmine brown 2 to blend the background into the halo. Then I refine the ridges in the carafe with blue-gray 5 and 7. To sharpen the lower edge of the carafe, I apply some bistre 3. Then I warm the light behind the left onion with yellow ochre 5. Next I draw the peel and stem with yellow ochre 3 and indicate the skin with English red light 3 and 5.

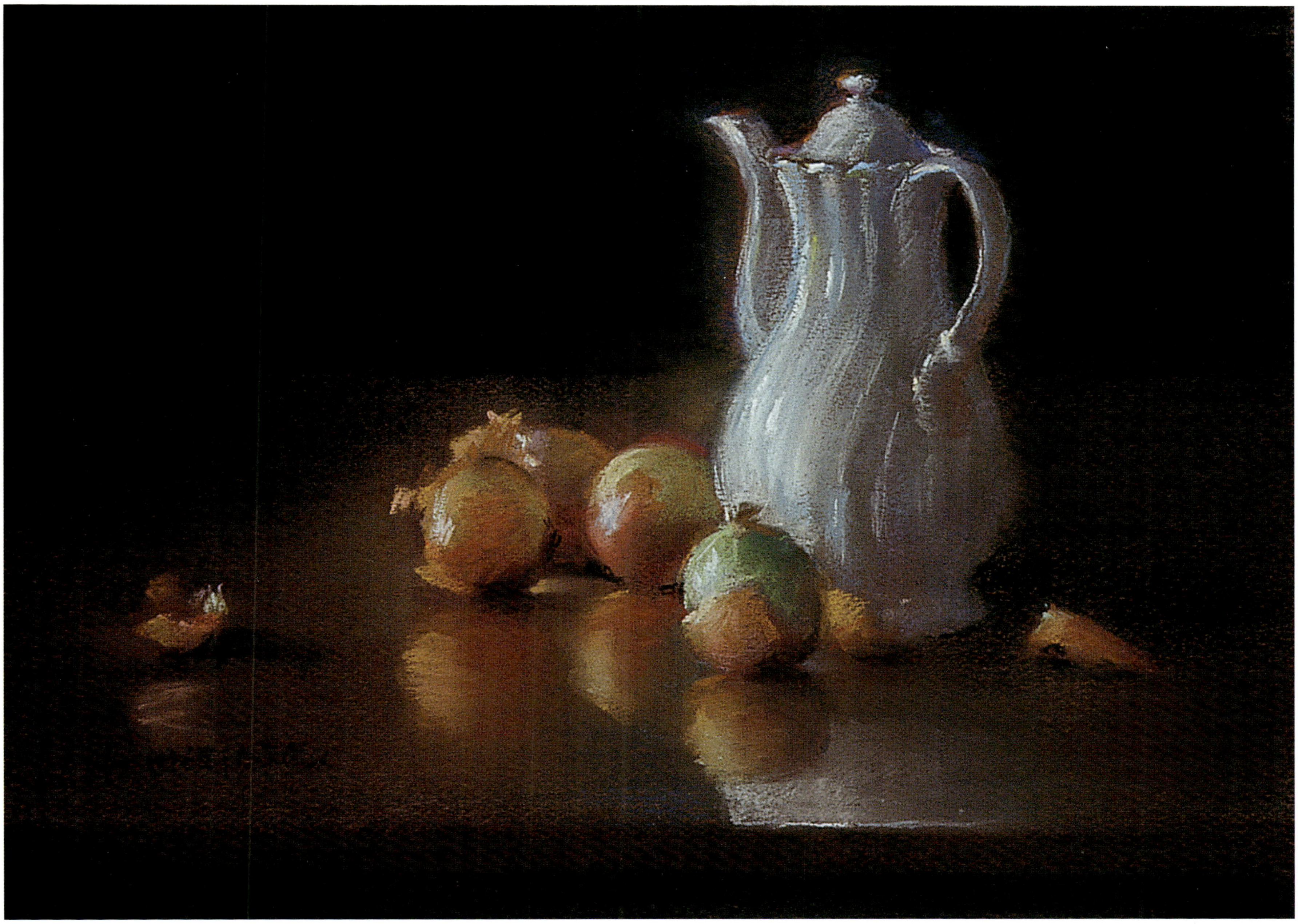

5 Now I refine and correct some of the edges on the carafe with madder brown 2 and brighten some of the highlights with cobalt blue 7. Then I sharpen some of the dark accents near the onions with burnt sienna 3. I add a final highlight of turquoise blue 9 on the edge of the table to make it appear to come forward a bit more and establish the foreground edge. After taking a step back and assessing my work, I'm confident that the finished piece conveys the original concept of the movement of light from right to left.

Creating Depth

One of the most rewarding things about painting a landscape is being able to create the illusion of depth and distance. I use a variety of visual cues to convey a sense of depth, but one of the most important is the use of atmospheric perspective. *Atmospheric perspective* refers to the fact that particles in the air—such as moisture and dust—block out some of the red wavelengths of light, so objects in the distance appear less distinct and cooler in value than those in the foreground. Therefore I paint the objects closest to me with the most texture, detail, and intense colors, and I use increasingly less detail and more muted colors for the objects that are farther away. I also suggest depth with a few other simple techniques, such as overlapping objects and painting nearer objects larger than those in the distance. In this rural landscape, I emphasized the texture and size of the warm and brightly colored hay bale and stubble in the foreground, overlapped the trees in the middle ground and background, and blurred the edges and smoothed the forms of the cool and distant fields, trees, and sky.

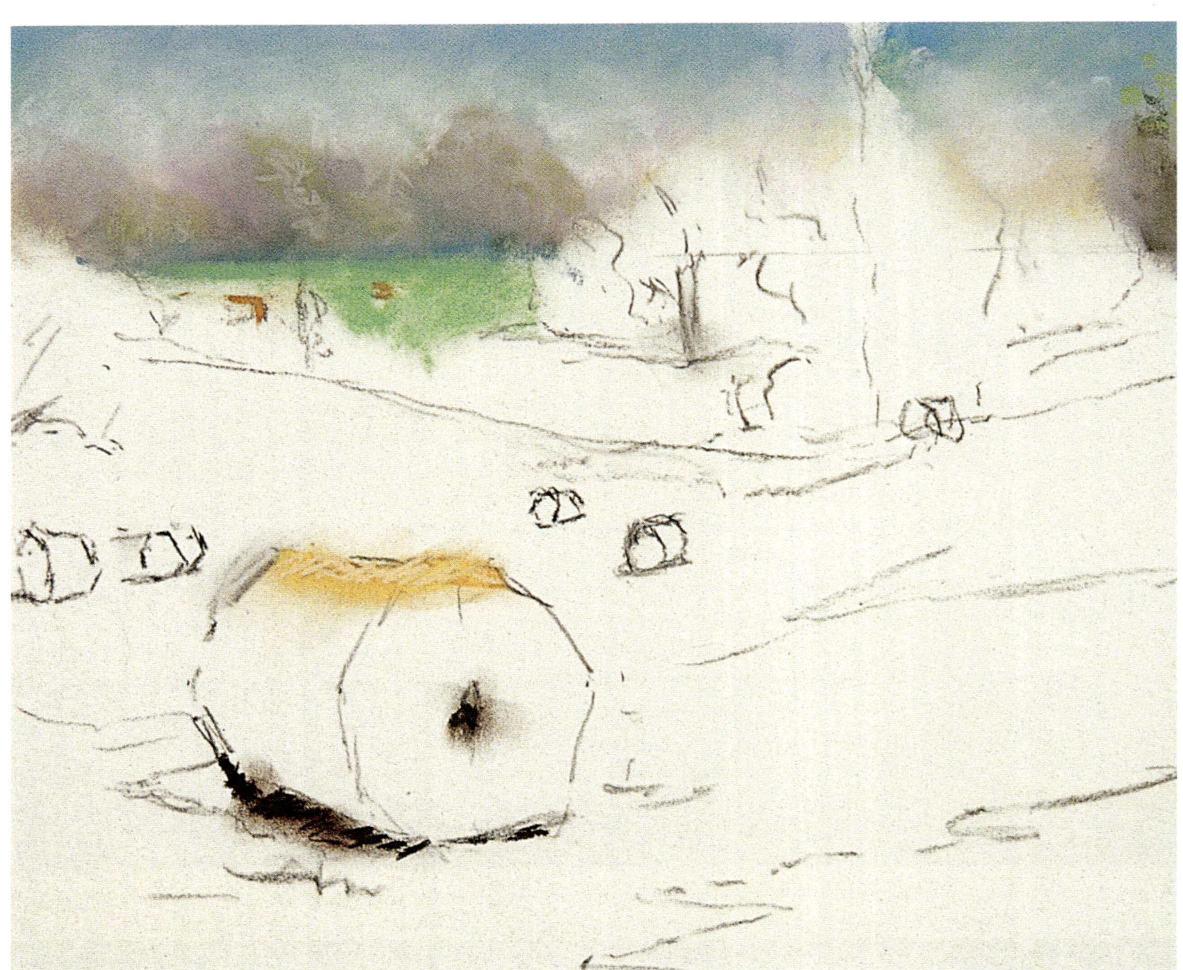

1 First I lay out my design with vine charcoal on an off-white sheet of sanded pastel paper. Then I establish the lightest light (the sunlight on top of the hay bale) with permanent red light 5, deep yellow 7, and orange 9. Next I lay in the darkest dark (the shadow underneath) with Mars violet 5 and black. It's important that the two value extremes are in the foreground of the painting; having the strongest contrasts in the foreground helps create the sense that this area is closest to the viewer. Now I begin to work from the back to the front, so I can easily overlap objects as I go. I lay in the sky with ultramarine blue 5, cobalt blue 7, and phthalo blue 9. Where the sky lightens near the horizon, I work in deep yellow 9, red-violet light 8, and permanent rose 10, blending these colors with the side of my hand. Then I use blue-gray 7, blue-violet 5, and olive green 8 for the distant row of trees, blending the strokes well with my palm.

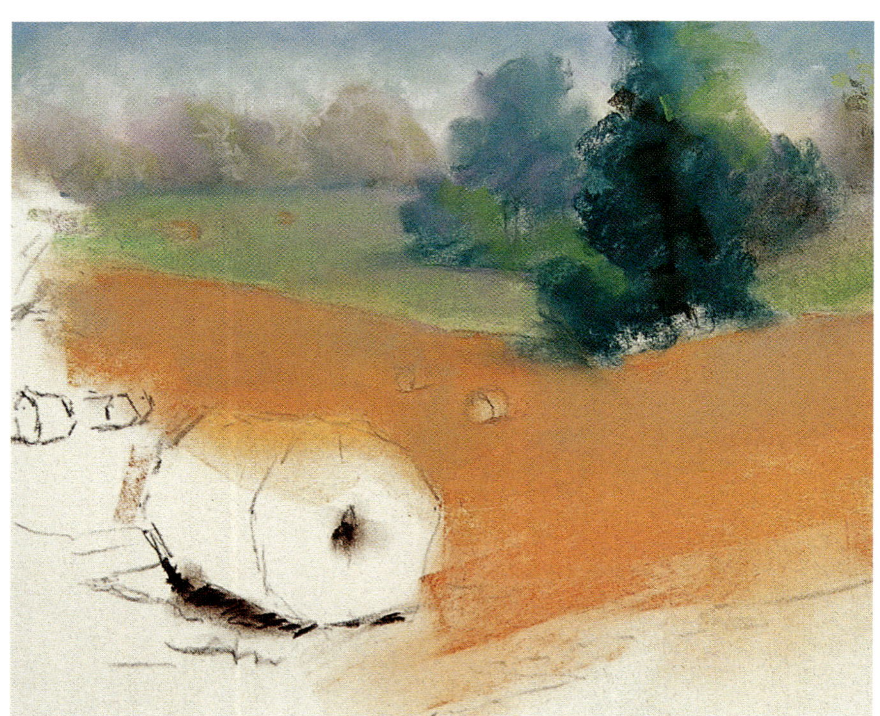

2 Working my way forward and blending virtually every stroke, I paint the distant grass with olive green 5, phthalo green 7, and red-violet deep 5. Remember that the atmosphere cools and grays things in the distance—the red-violet I use cools and neutralizes the greens. For the middle trees, I use red-violet deep 5, olive green 5, blue-green 5, and gray 5. The two overlapping trees closest to the viewer are blocked in with red-violet deep 3 and blue-green 3, while their dark shadows are bistre 3. For the red of the mowed field, I use burnt sienna 5, red-violet 5, and gray 8.

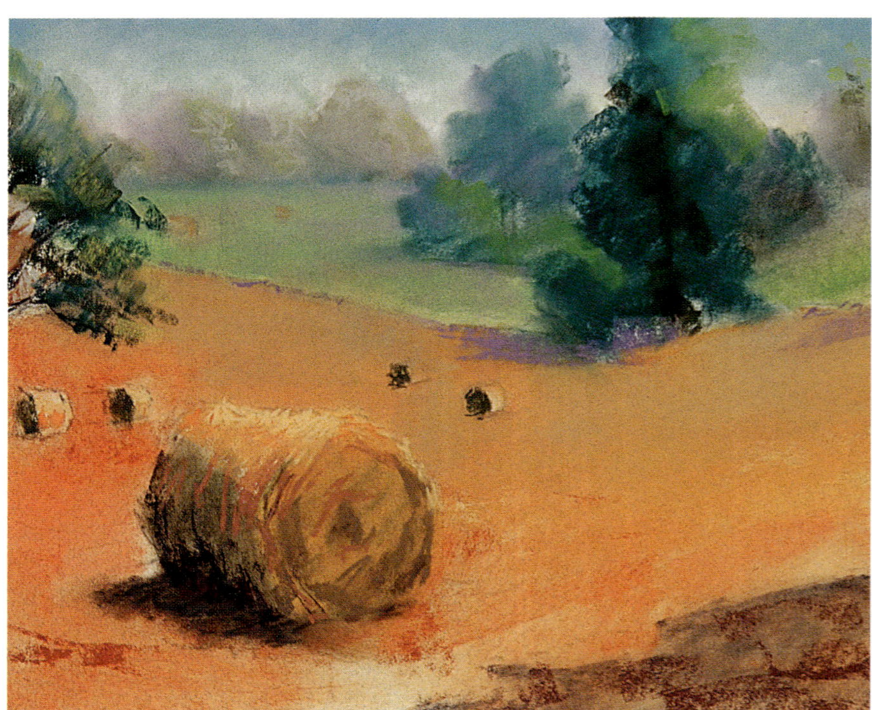

3 Next I paint the shadows of the middle trees with red-violet 5 and blue-violet 3. The shadows on the smaller hay bales are olive green 5 and burnt sienna 5. For the shadowed side of the foreground bale, I use olive green 3, light oxide red 3, and orange 3. Then I render the end of the bale with caput mortuum red 7, permanent red light 5, and gold ochre 5, blending these strokes less so the details are sharper. I establish a base tone for the foreground with scarlet 5 and burnt sienna 5, and I use caput mortuum red 3 and red-violet 3 for the shadow on the near right. Then I paint the left tree with chrome green deep 3, olive green 5, and deep yellow 5.

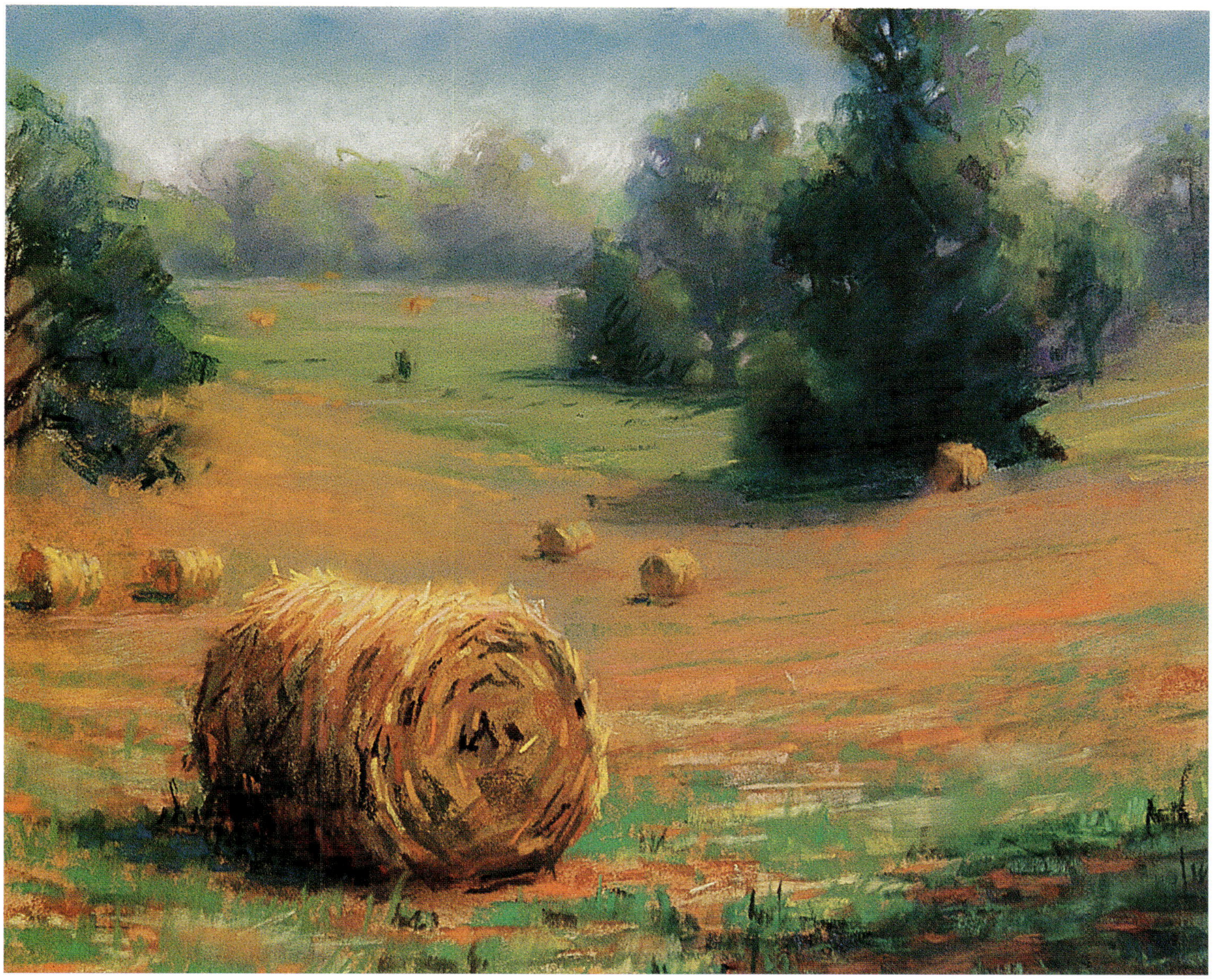

6 To finish, I add a number of unblended strokes to the foreground so that it is the area of most texture and detail. I place some gold ochre 9 highlights to indicate the pieces of mown hay lying on the ground. Then I work some burnt sienna 5 to suggest the ground in the spaces between the shadowed grass patches. For the highlights in the grass and on the hay bale, I use chrome green 10 and deep yellow 5 and 7. Finally I add a few more dark strokes in the hay bale with raw umber 3—and I'm done!

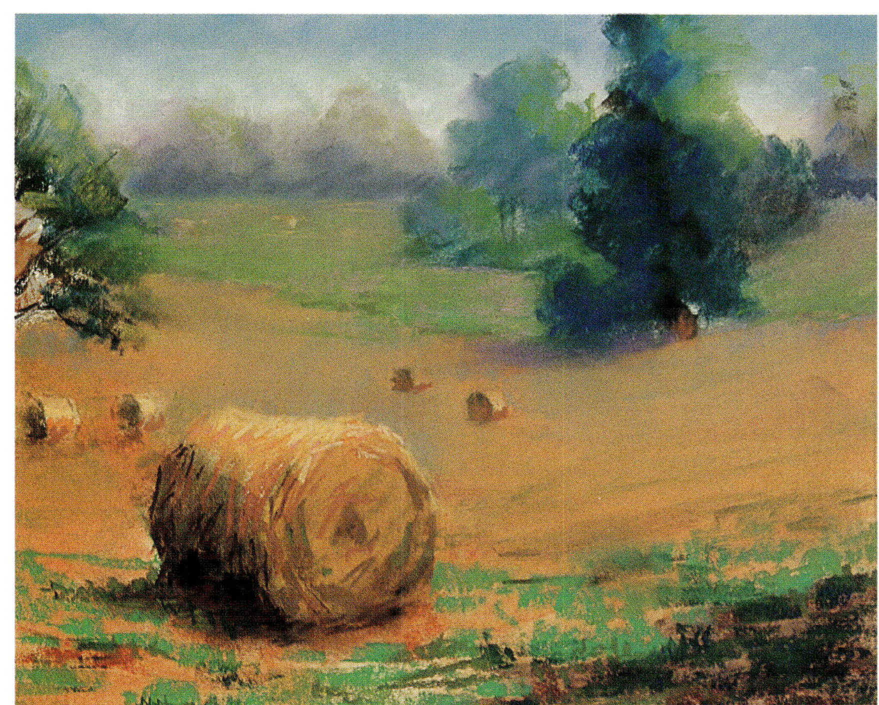

4 Now I step back and study the overall effect of my painting. I decide that I need to gray the field slightly with blue-gray 7 to contrast with the bright color of the foreground hay bale and make it "pop" forward. Then I paint the foreground grass with chrome green 5 and phthalo green 5. I also use chrome green deep 5 to add some grass into the shadows. Next I work olive green 5 and 8 into the distant fields and then overlay strokes of red-violet 7 to create the hazy effect of atmosphere. Then I adjust the distant row of trees with blue-gray 5 and cobalt blue 5, using blue-purple 5 for the shadow areas.

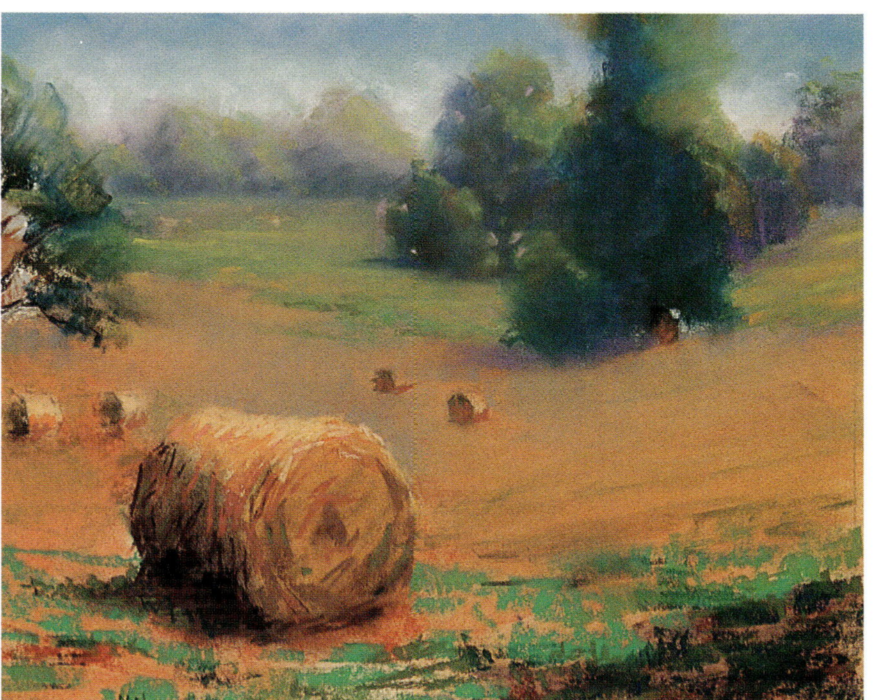

5 Now that most of the groundwork has been laid, I add the look of sunlight on the distant trees by applying olive green 8. Then I darken the middle ground trees with ultramarine blue 5 and blue-violet 5 and add the sunlit areas with olive green 8, orange 5, and mouse gray 5. I define the shape of the trunk using olive green 8 to paint the area around it rather than actually painting the trunk itself. (This is referred to as "painting the *negative spaces*"; the trunk and foliage are the *positive shapes,* and the spaces between and around them are the *negative shapes.*)

Expressing Mood

Color has a tremendous effect on people. Whether subtle or strong, color affects our feelings and arouses our emotions. Warm colors—such as reds, yellows, and oranges—convey energy and excitement, and cool colors—like greens, blues, and purples— tend to be more calming. Muted, grayed tones also have a soothing effect. Knowing how colors relate to and interact with one another will help you express an array of emotions—as well as interest and unity—in your paintings. For example, in this landscape, I want the viewer to experience the peaceful serenity of the fog-shrouded dawn, which I will convey through a toned-down palette. So before I begin painting, I determine what the dominant value and color will be. In this case, the values and colors are subdued by the mist, so the dominant value is a light middle tone, and the dominant color is a muted yellow-red with complementary touches of grayed purple and green. To enhance the peaceful mood and color harmony, I use both neutralized and lighter values of these colors throughout the painting.

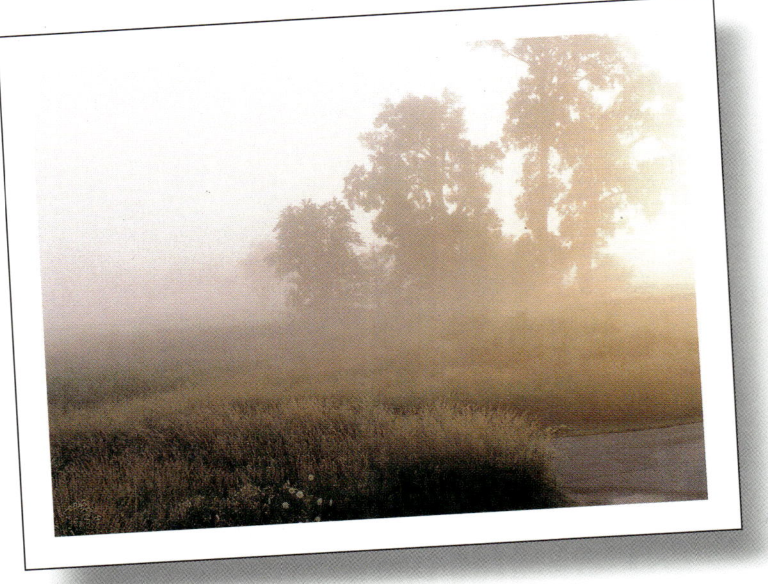

TAKING PHOTOGRAPHS If you are unable to paint on site, taking good reference photos is the next best alternative. (For more on painting outdoors, see page 30.) When I painted this scene in my studio, referring to the photo made it easy to recapture the way I felt when I first saw this sunrise and took this shot.

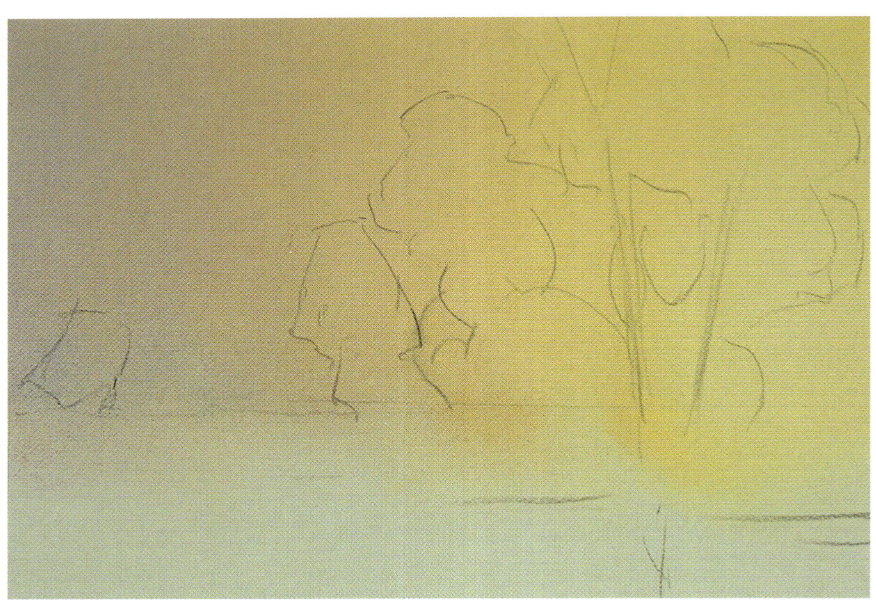

1 For this painting, I chose a light, warm-colored paper that will complement the dominant tone and value of the painting. (See page 20 for more on choosing colored papers.) I begin by laying the base color of the sky, starting with warmer colors on the right. I use light yellow 5 and deep yellow 5 and 9, gradually transitioning to permanent red 5 and carmine 7. As I work toward the left side, I add in some cooler colors (red-violet 7 and blue-violet 8). Next I sketch in the general placement of the trees with vine charcoal. Note that I counterbalance the mass of trees on the right with the small, solitary tree on the left. The balance of forms and the absence of strong diagonals in this composition reinforce the peaceful mood I want to impart.

2 Next I block in the general tones for the silhouetted trees, creating a warm-to-cool transition of color. As usual at this stage, I blend virtually every stroke with the side of my hand. This works the pastel into the paper, keeps the layer thin, and creates many soft edges. I start with orange 5 and chrome green 10 on the right and then move to red-violet 7 and olive green 5 and 8 in the middle. Then I use red-violet 7, blue-violet 5, and olive green 5 on the left side of the tree mass. I establish the cooler, darker mass in the foreground using olive green 3, blue-green 3, burnt sienna 3, and blue-violet 5. Be sure to pay attention to the color temperature relationship between light and shadow; in general, a warm light source will cast cool shadows.

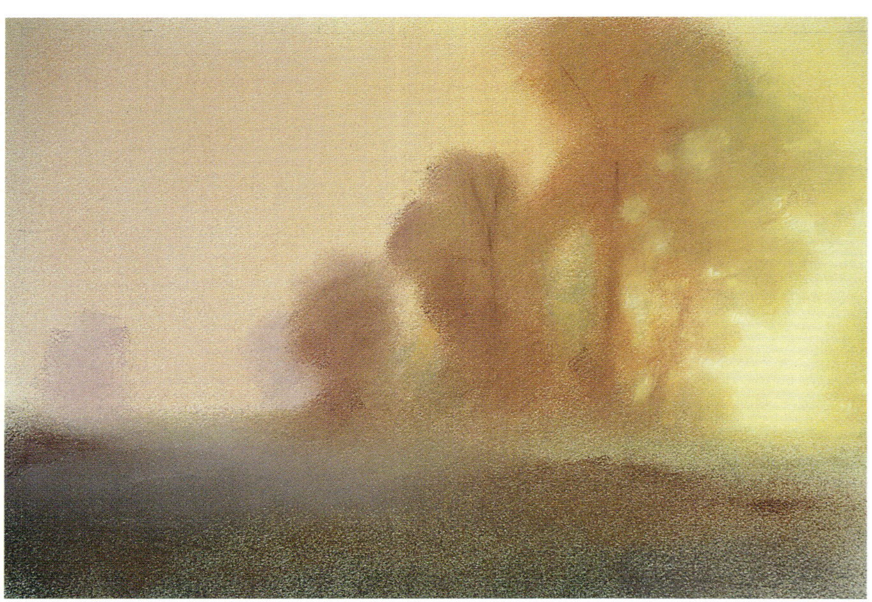

3 Next I indicate the trunks of the trees with Indian red 3 and 5. Starting on the right, I begin to paint in the "sky holes" (the negative spaces in the foliage where the sky is visible) using deep yellow 7 and 9. With pastel, it is often easier to create a solid tone for the tree and then paint the negative spaces on top, rather than the other way around. But you need to be careful of the edges; if they're too hard, the sky may seem to pop forward in front of the trees. Also keep in mind that, even though we know the sky is all the same value, these sky holes appear to be darker than the sky itself—perhaps because small twigs are diffusing the light, or perhaps because the eye just perceives them to be darker. In any event, paint them a darker value.

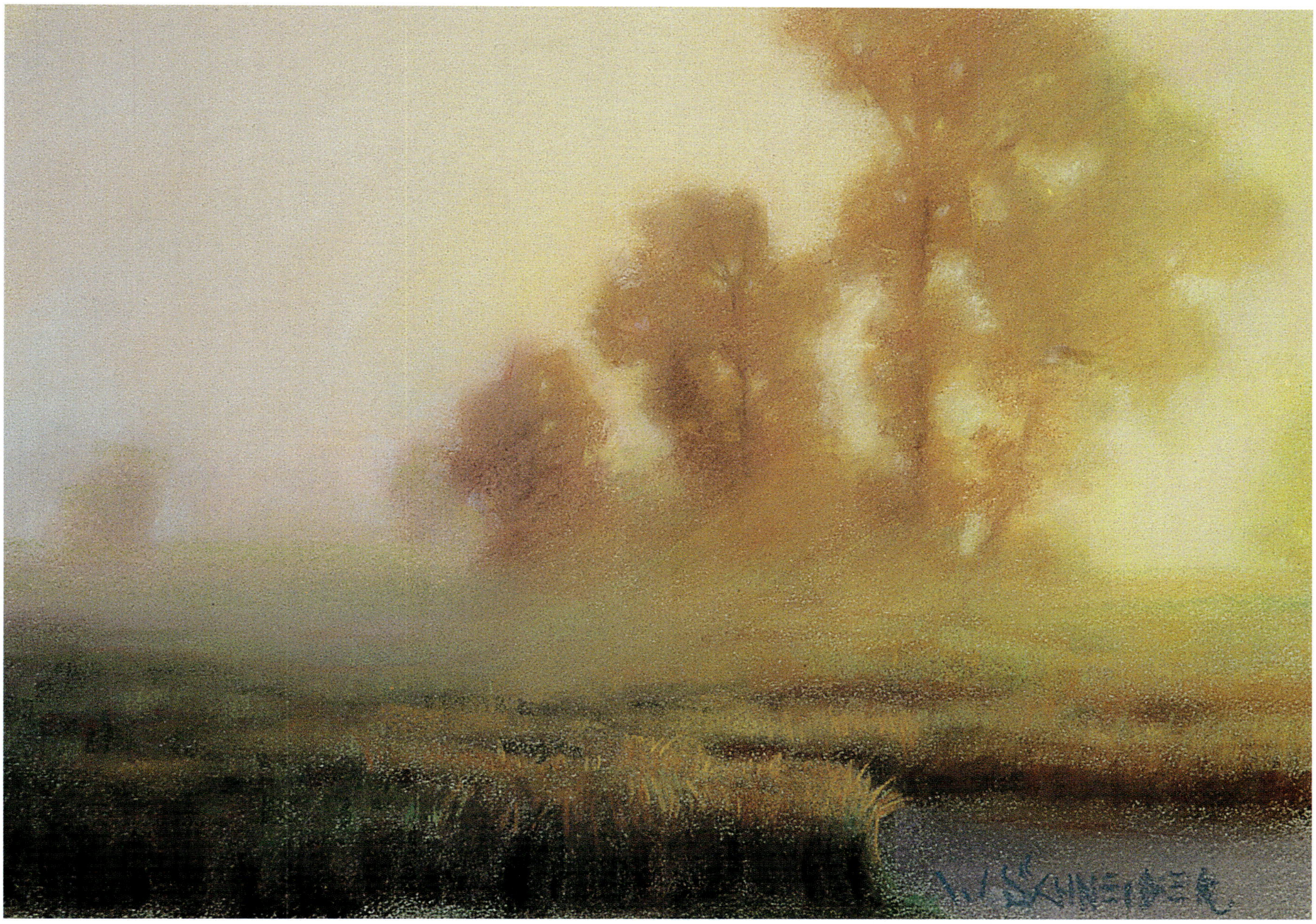

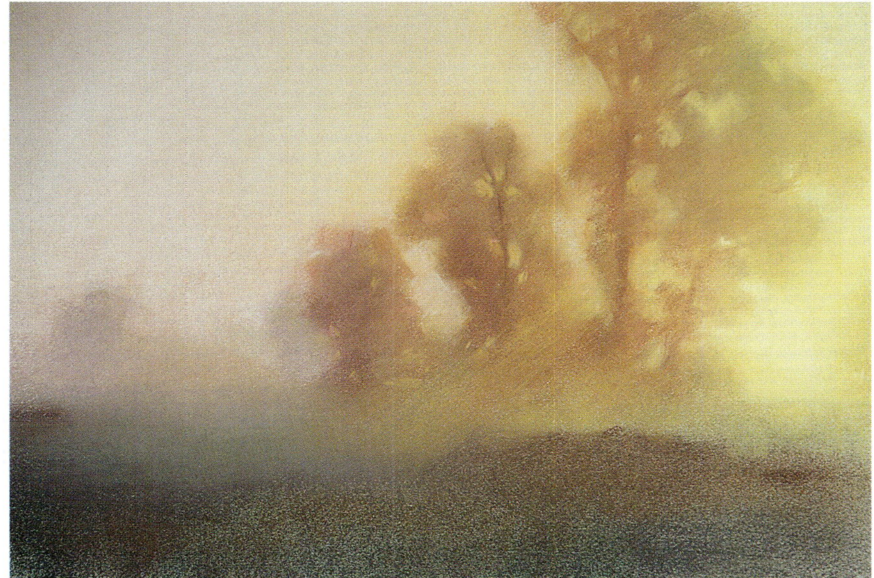

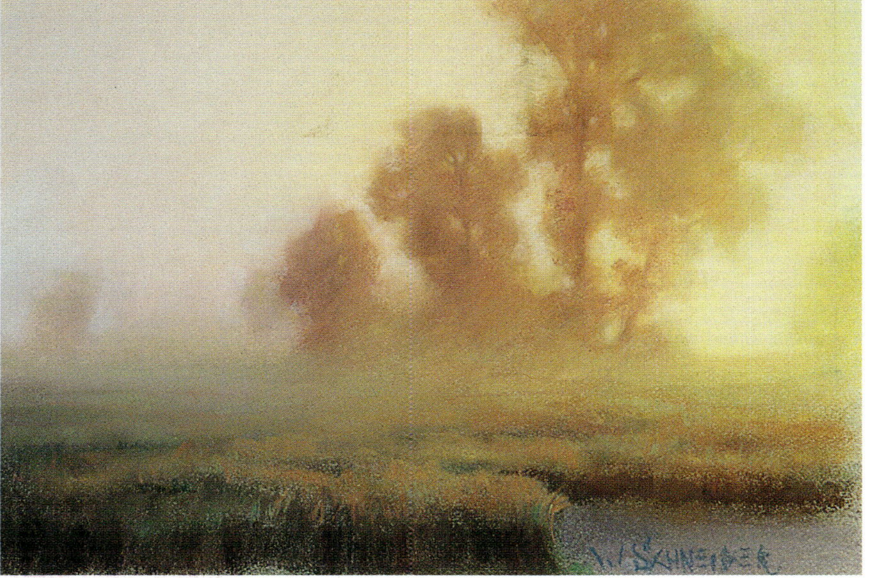

6 After living with the painting for a day or two, I decide that I need to sharpen the image a bit to create a greater visual impact. To increase the contrast, I lighten the sky on the right with orange 9 and white. I lighten the sky on the left side with a well-blended layer of Mars violet 10.

Then I paint in a few smaller sky holes into the trees using English red 7 and deep yellow 7. Next I darken the foreground with bistre 7, burnt sienna 3 and 5, and olive green 3. Finally I add a few sharp strokes of orange 5 and 3 to depict individual grass stalks that are illuminated by the sun.

4 In this step, I lighten and gray the sky with the complements of blue-violet deep 9 and deep yellow 7. I choose these complements for this reason: Particles of pastel pigment often lie adjacent to one another, rather than covering one another completely, as usually happens with paint. Because they are side by side, the complements resonate visually, and this creates a luminous effect. Then I drag some yellow deep 5 over the trees to indicate light streaming into the mist. The rich color not only helps create the effect of light, but the diagonal strokes also add little bit of action to the composition. Next I use some well-blended strokes of phthalo green 8 and blue-violet 8 to indicate the middle ground mist on the left side.

5 Next I complete the foreground. The darkest values are in the front: red-violet 3, burnt sienna 3, and black. I use a light touch of denatured alcohol and a brush to solidify those darks. Then I indicate some of the grasses with olive green 5 and chrome green 5. I use strokes of burnt sienna 5, caput mortuum red 5, and orange 5 to indicate the tops of the grasses that are bathed in the warm light of the rising sun. Note that the trees have almost no detail. They exist primarily as silhouettes against the sky. We know a lot about an object by its shape. For example, if you see a tree from a great distance, you can recognize its type by its silhouette long before you see its leaves. Satisfied with my painting, I sign my name.

Rendering Light with Value

I think light is one of the most important and fascinating elements in a painting. Although you can't actually paint light itself, you can capture the effect of light by using both value and color temperature contrasts, such as placing light and dark values next to each other and pairing warm colors with cool colors. The contrast in value doesn't have to be dramatic; in fact, if the extremes (the darkest and lightest colors) are closer in value, your painting will seem more realistic. But contrasts in color temperature—between the warm, light areas and the cool shadows—have a great impact. In this outdoor scene, for example, I played up the contrast between the red and yellow light and the blue and green shadows. Notice that the warm-colored adobe dwelling appears to be intensely lit not only because it is bathed in warm light, but also because it is placed against the cool colors of the blue background hills.

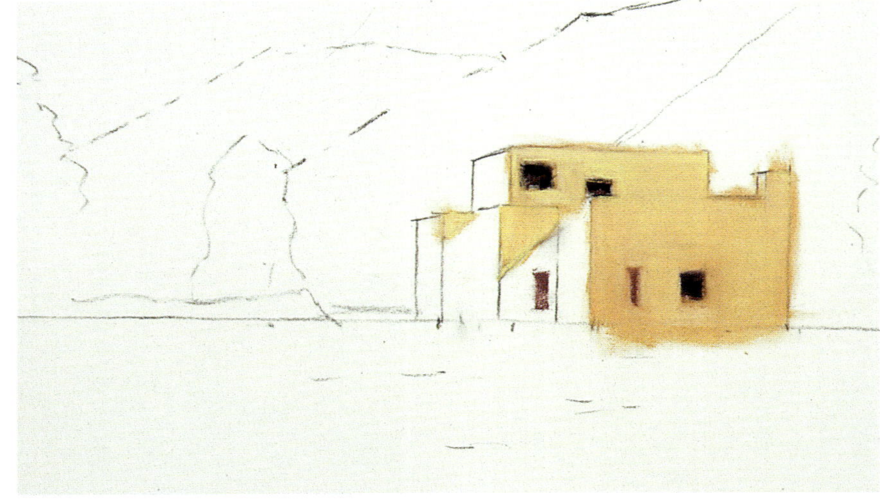

1 First I sketch the scene on off-white, sanded pastel board. (I chose off-white so my lightest values would appear rich and dark against the paper.) Next I paint the lightest value—the sunlit adobe walls—with a blend of permanent red 5, orange 5, and gold ochre 7. Then I paint the darkest value (the window) with a combination of bistre 3, carmine brown 2, and gray-green 3. In this painting, there are only about four value steps between the lightest and darkest values.

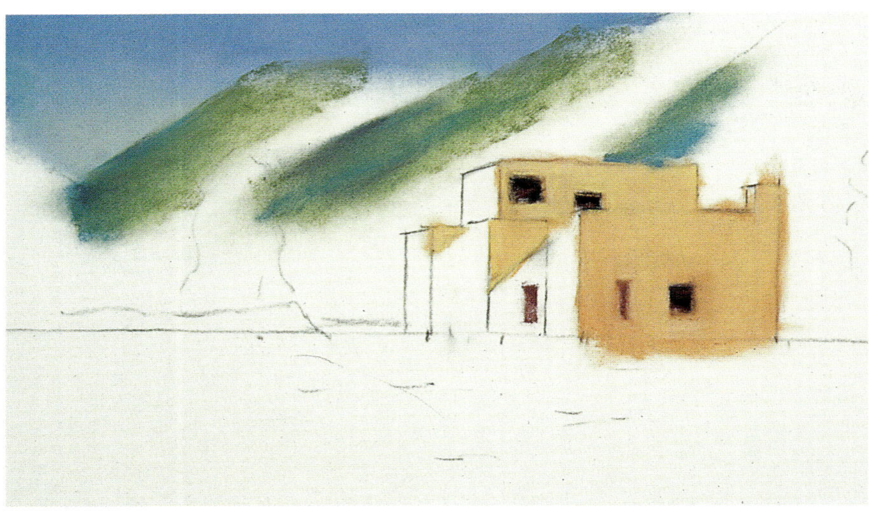

2 I want to establish some of the contrasting cool colors right away, so I paint the sky with a blend of turquoise blue 5, cobalt blue 5 and 7, and ultramarine blue 7, with phthalo blue 9 near the horizon. Note that the sky is not only cooler but also slightly darker than the house. Then I use olive green 5 and turquoise blue 5 for the shadows on the hills.

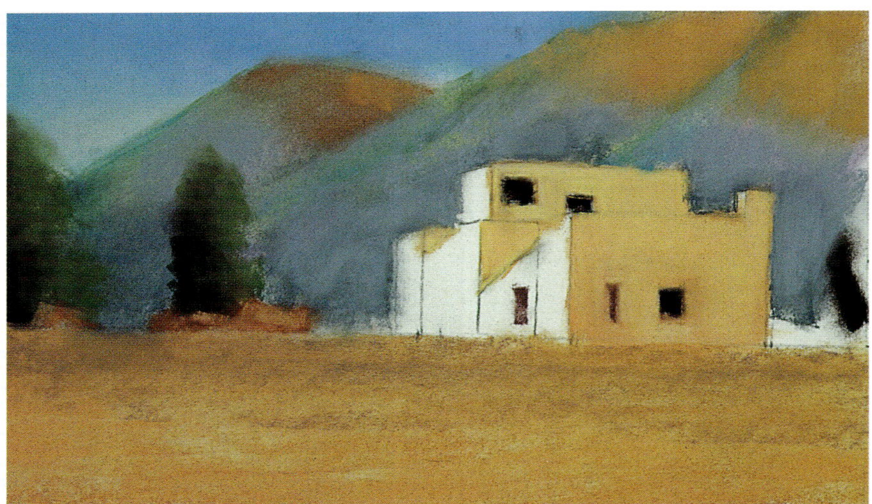

3 I use gray 5 and blue-gray 7 to block in the mountains, blue-violet 5 for the distant hill, and carmine brown 3 for the shadowed trees. For the light on the hills, I blend orange 3 and permanent red 5 into the cooler gray tones. Next I paint the foreground with orange 3 and blue-violet 5 near the horizon.

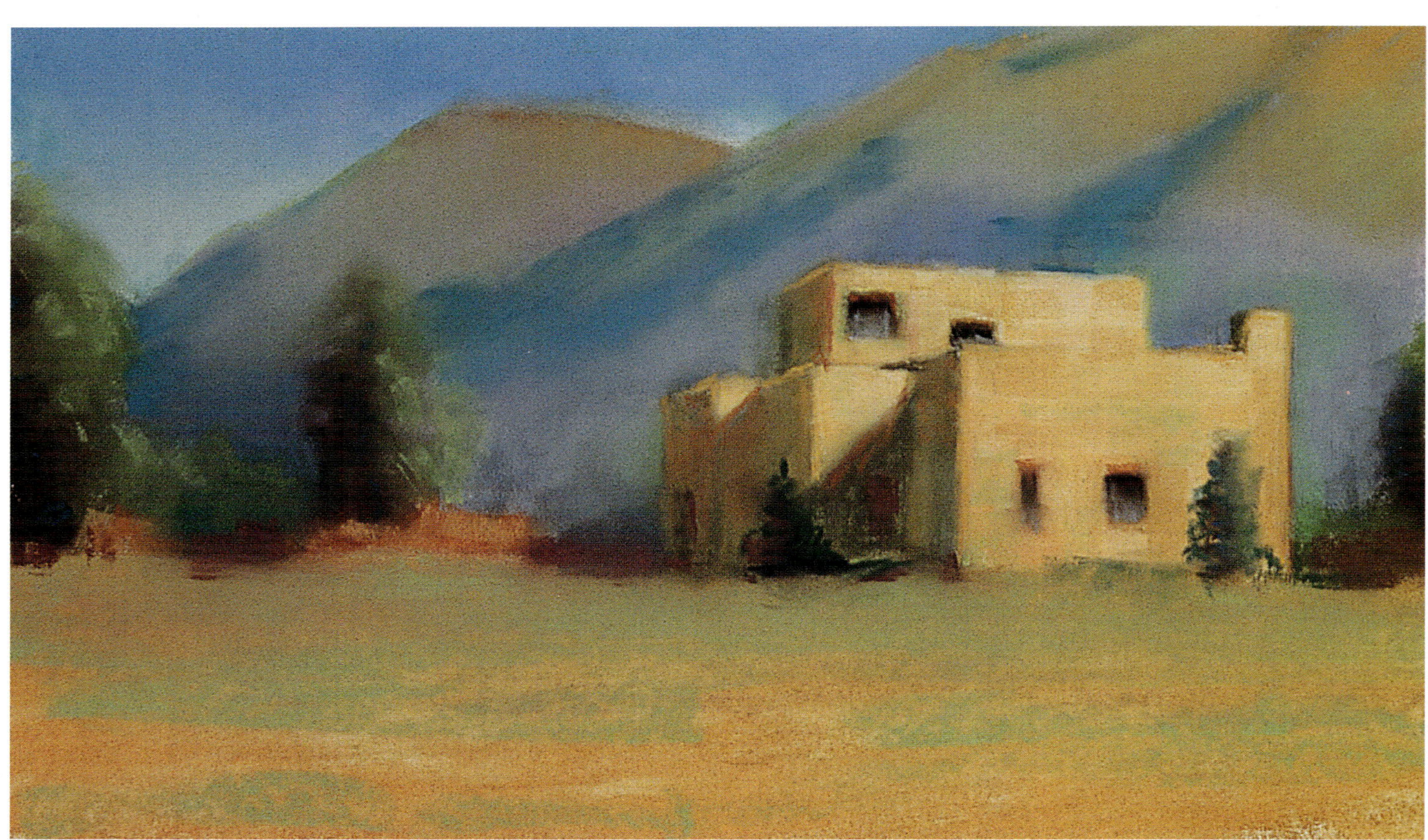

4 Next I paint the shadows on the house with olive green 3 and orange 3 and refine the shadows on the mountains with blue-gray 5 and turquoise blue 5. I paint the light areas of the trees with olive green 7, adding some of the same color to the ground, and I apply carmine brown 3 and chrome green deep 5 to the trees by the house. Then I warm the shadows on the adobe with burnt sienna 5—particularly on the edge between light and shadow—and define the edges of the adobe house more clearly with gold ochre 5. Then I lighten the shadows on the hills with Prussian blue 7 and redraw their edges with turquoise blue 3. For the shadowy darks on either side of the house, I use Indian red 3.

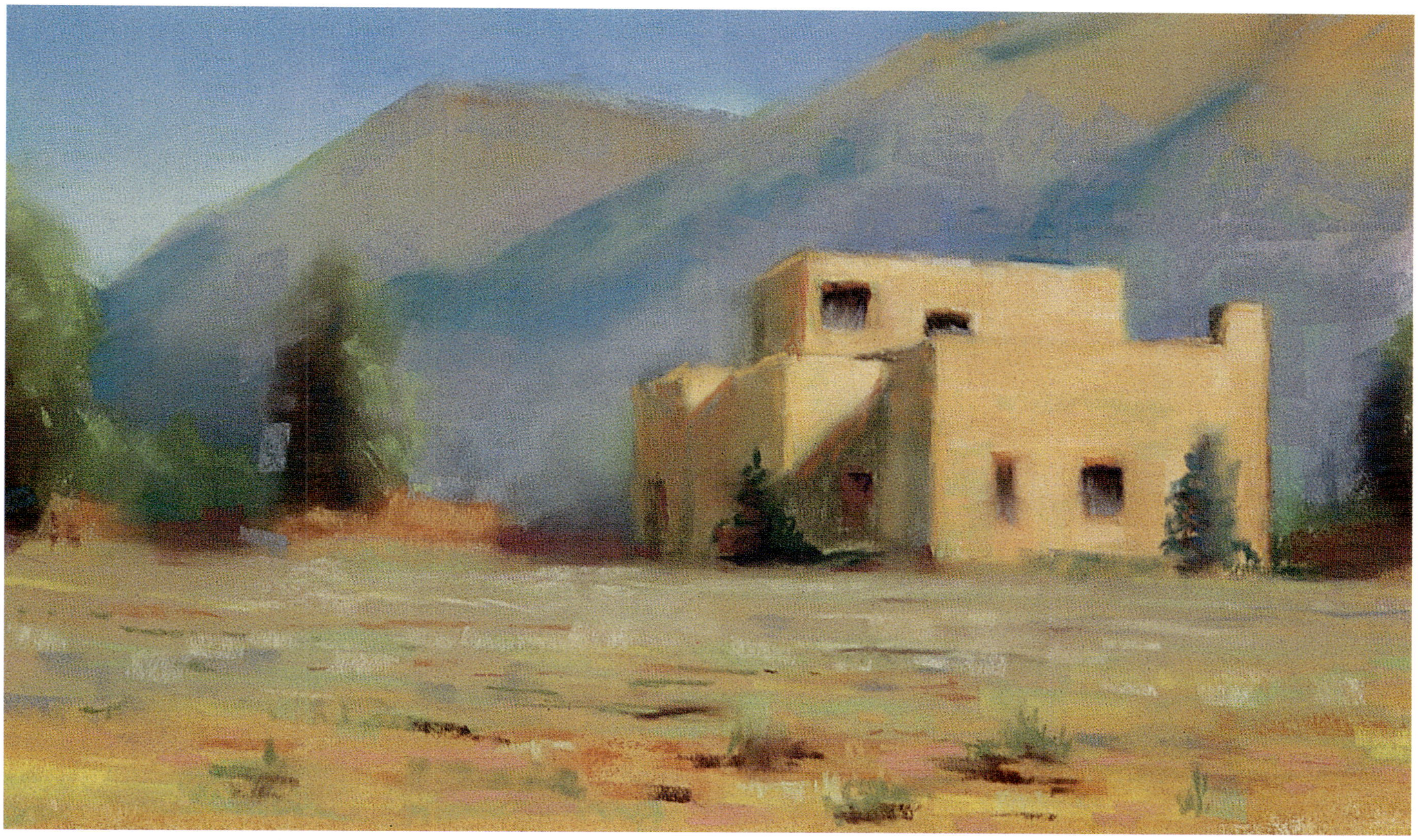

5 Now I begin to indicate some of the texture in the foreground with burnt sienna 3 and yellow ochre 3 and 5. To create the effect of sparse vegetation on the desert floor, I add different shapes of olive green 5, gold ochre 3, chrome green 7, lemon yellow 7, and light English red 7.

Adding texture to the foreground makes that plane seem to come forward, and I also use these spots of vegetation to draw the viewer's eye into the painting and direct it toward my center of interest: the adobe house.

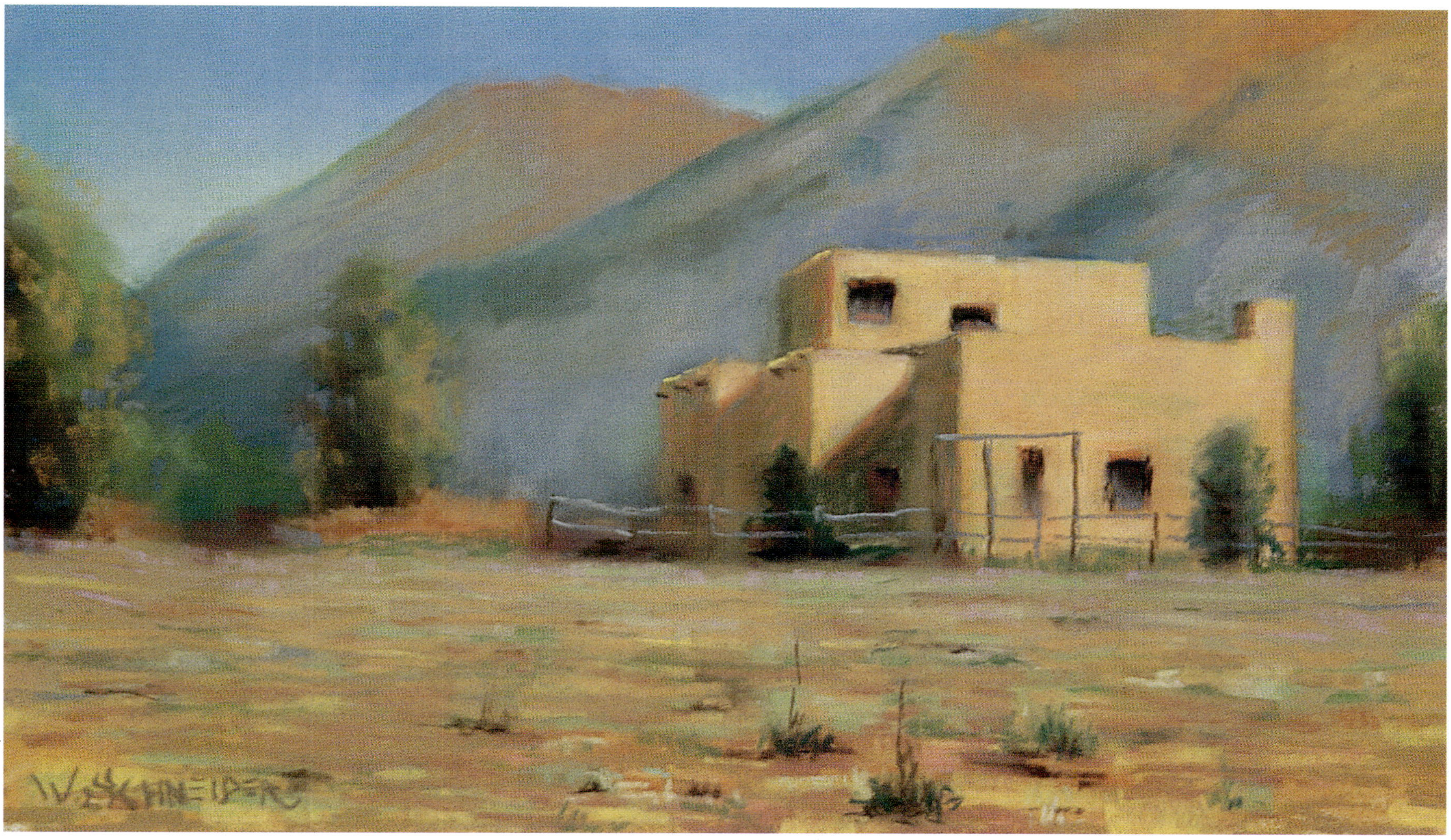

6 Next I sharpen some of the edges in the shadowed windows with purple 3. Then I add a hint of autumn color in the trees with orange 3. I draw the fence posts with burgundy 3 and indicate the fence rails with mouse gray 5. The details I place in the foreground plants helps the rest of the color shapes "read" as vegetation. In general, if you show a few details, the viewer's mind will fill in the rest. Then I step back to assess my work and notice that I drew the windows and the chimney with a slight lean, so I correct those lines. I also straighten the alignment on the top of the house by painting in some of the hill color. Then I add a few dark accents to the house and the surrounding trees, and the painting is complete.

Portraying Animals

Animals are interesting, engaging, and often exciting painting subjects. Whether an energetic puppy, a lumbering bear, or a graceful elk, an animal provides a wide range of shapes, lines, and textures to intrigue an artist. And painting animals is just like painting anything else—all you need to do is see shapes of color and put them in the correct place on your paper. But when painting animals, I also want to capture the unique qualities of my subject, such as the animal's skin or hair texture and its features and body type. For an artist, the biggest challenge may be finding a model that will sit still enough for you to paint it, but movement is what adds life to your paintings. Consult books or magazines for appealing photographs, or take pictures of your pet. Look for subtle types of movement, like the twist of my cat Molly's body and the direction of her gaze in this painting. Don't worry if your rendition doesn't look exactly like your subject—a painting of an animal doesn't have to be a perfect likeness to be appreciated.

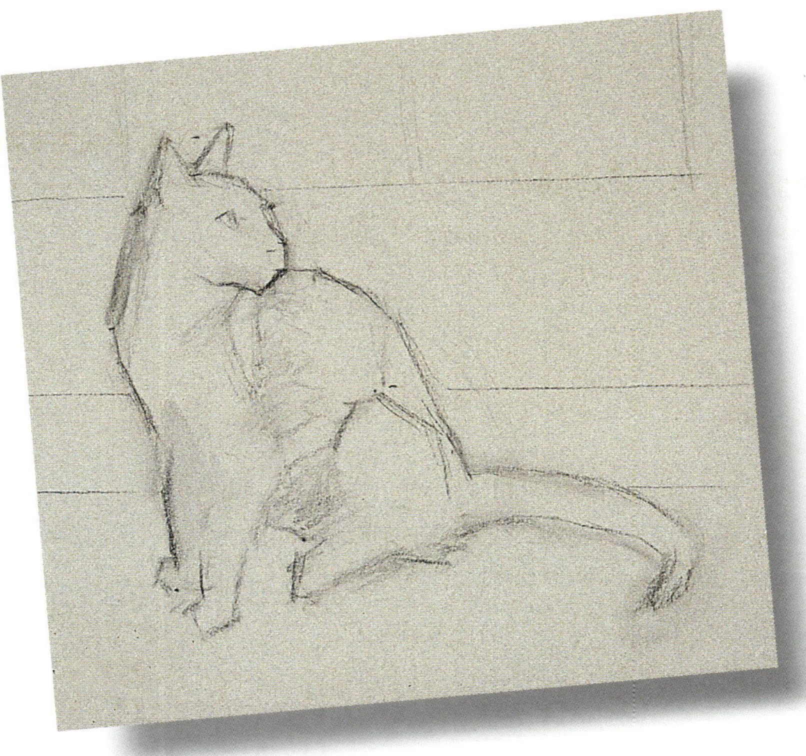

SKETCHING THE BASIC SHAPES The design of this painting is relatively simple: My cat Molly is silhouetted against the light of a patio door so I don't have to worry about extraneous elements or distracting details in the surrounding scene. I begin by drawing Molly's main shapes and roughing out her outlines, then by sketching the lines of the glass and wood door. Note that the pose shows a lot of movement even though the cat is sitting still. (See page 22 for more on movement and the line of action.)

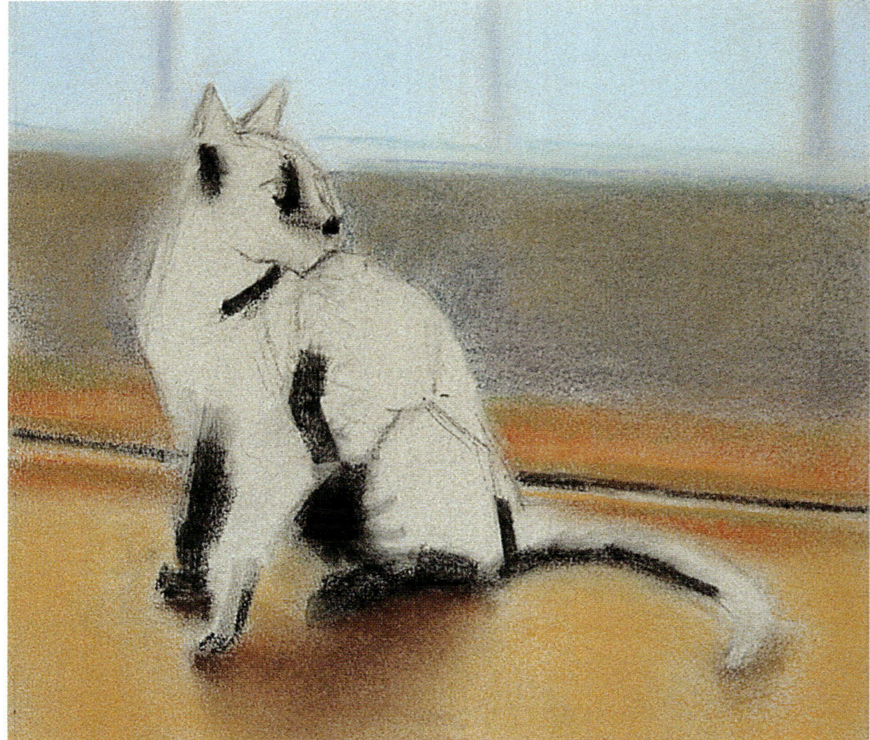

1 First I establish the light area of the window with cobalt blue 9. Then I mix black with denatured alcohol and paint the darks in the fur with a brush. Since I want to be able to blend the softness of the cat's fur into the surroundings, I paint the background first. I render the wall with blue-gray 5 and gold ochre 5, blending them well with my hand. Then I use burnt sienna 5, and chrome green 5 for the molding. The basic tone of the floor is gold ochre 5. Next I block in the shadow of the cat on the floor with light English red 3, carmine brown 5, and burnt sienna 5.

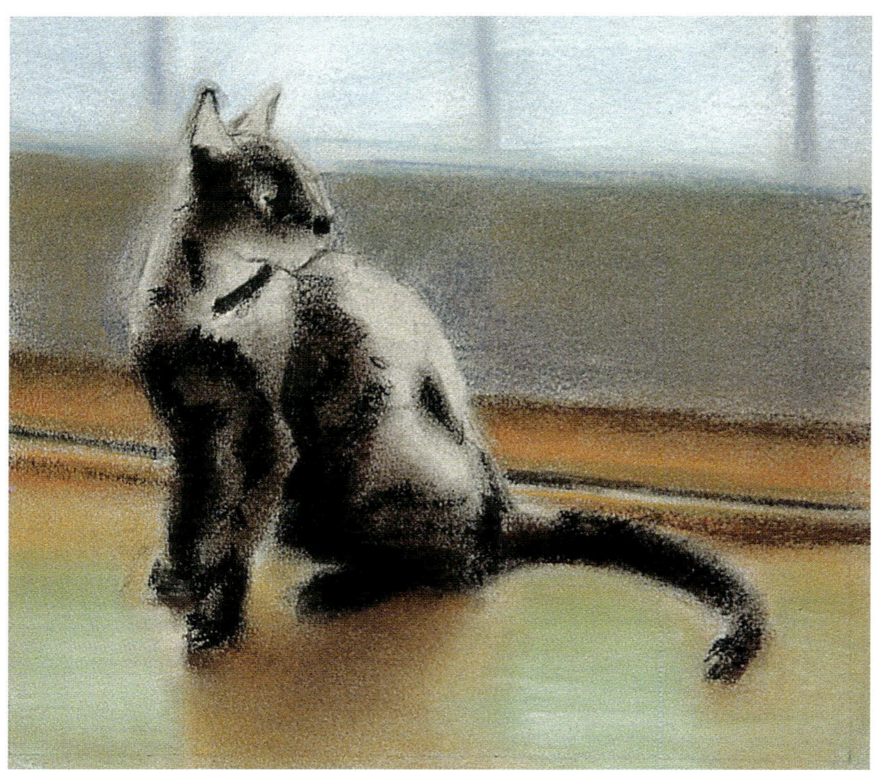

2 I lighten the floor with phthalo green 8, red-violet deep 9, and phthalo blue 9 to show the reflected light from the door. Then I lighten the value on the window with permanent rose 10, and I use carmine 3 for the dark of the molding. Now I'm ready to establish the shadow areas on the cat: I use a well-blended mix of carmine brown 3 and bistre 3 for the lighter colors in the fur, and I use black for the deepest shadows in the black fur.

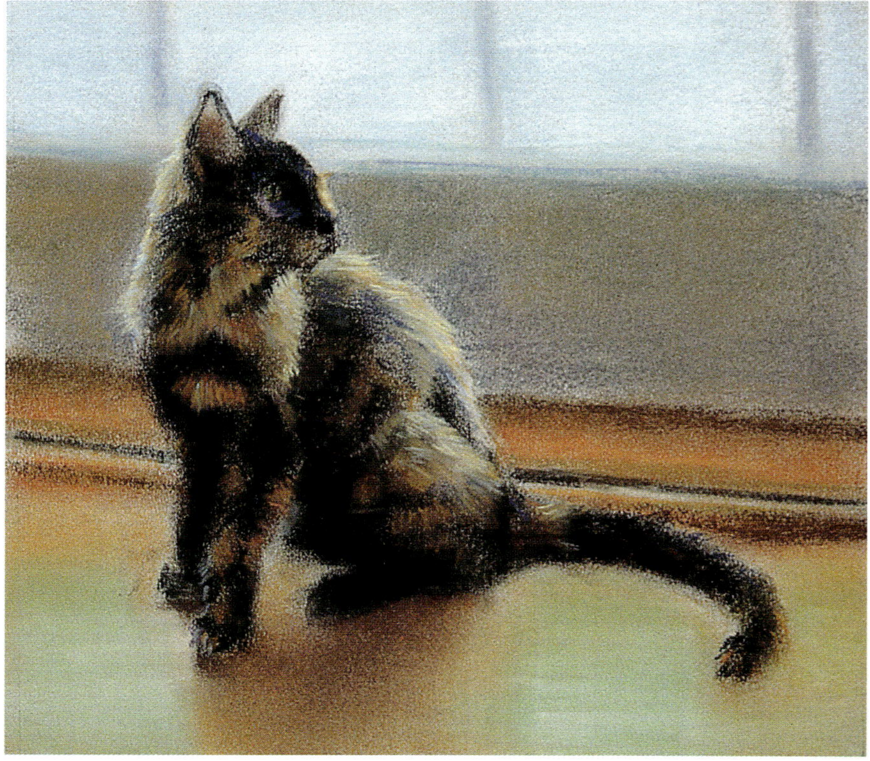

3 Next I use raw sienna 5 to paint the shadows in the lighter areas of fur, making unblended strokes that follow the direction of the fur growth. For the eye, I begin by painting the pupil black; then I draw around it with chrome green 5 grayed with scarlet 5 (its complement), touching lightly with my finger to soften the strokes. Next I use caput mortuum red 7 for the warm color in the ear, and I use gold ochre 5, gold ochre 7, and yellow ochre 7 for the highlighted fur.

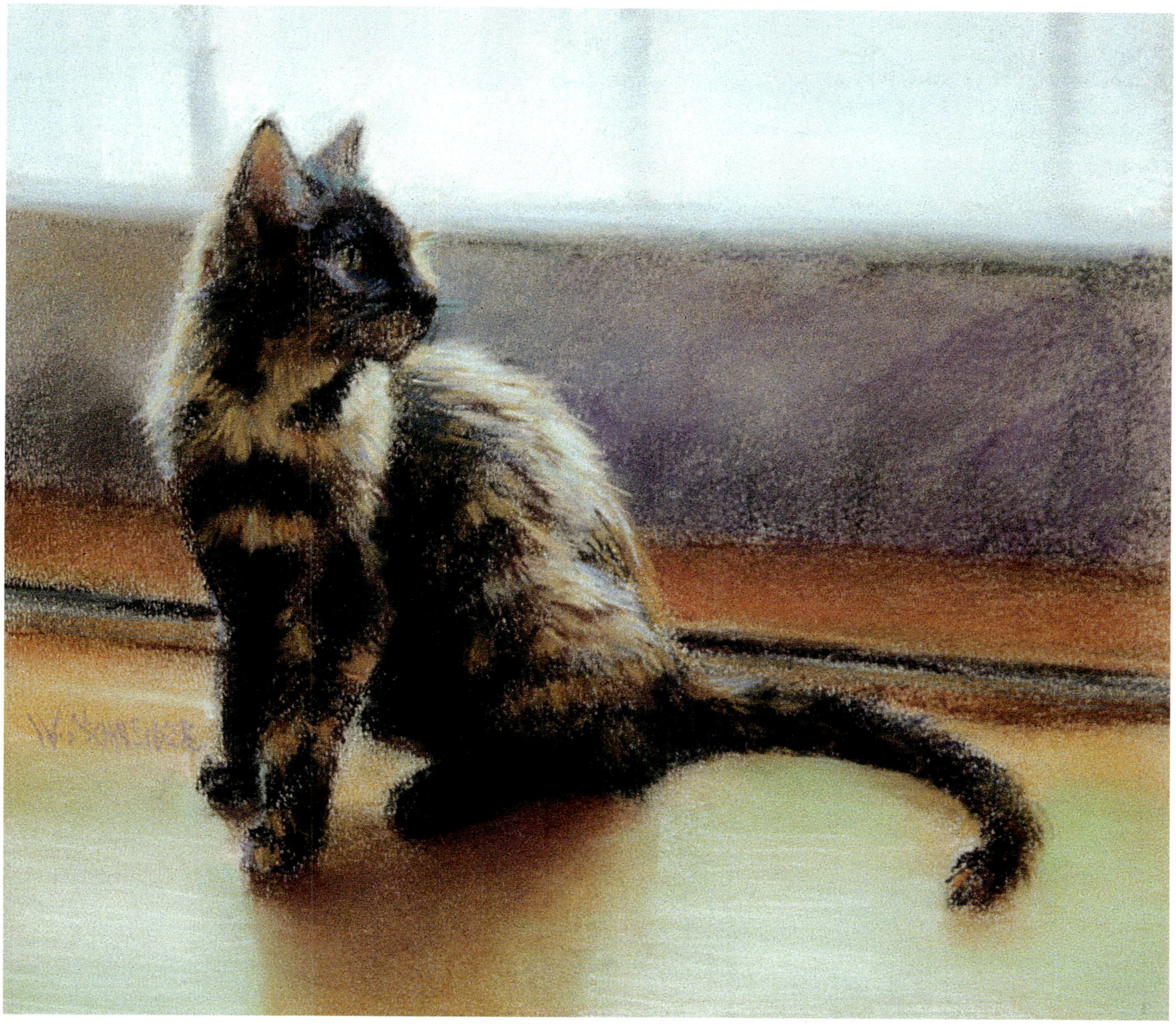

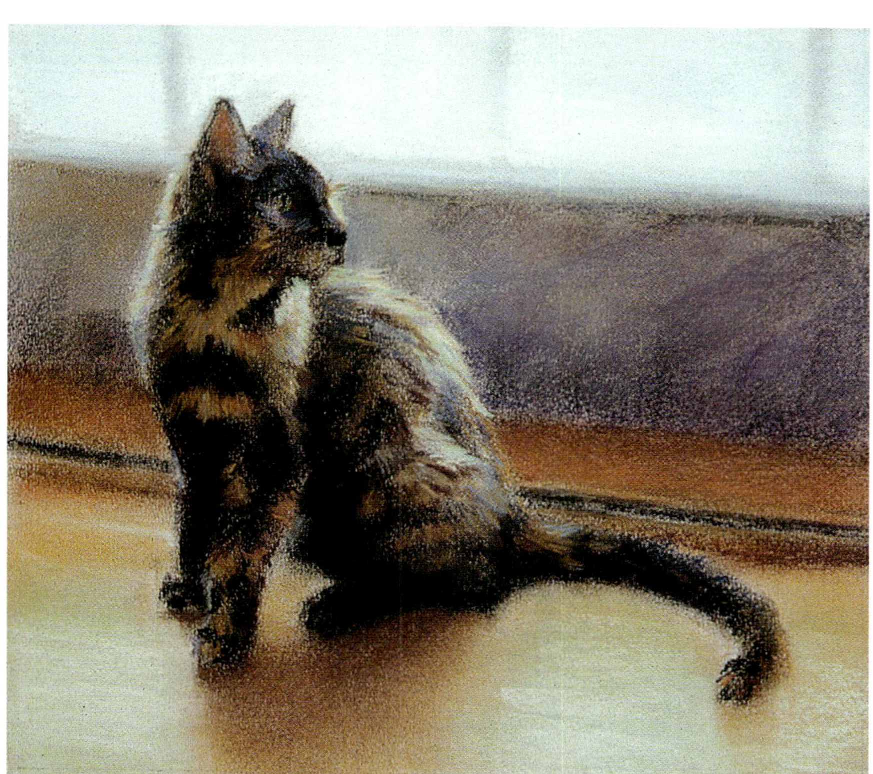

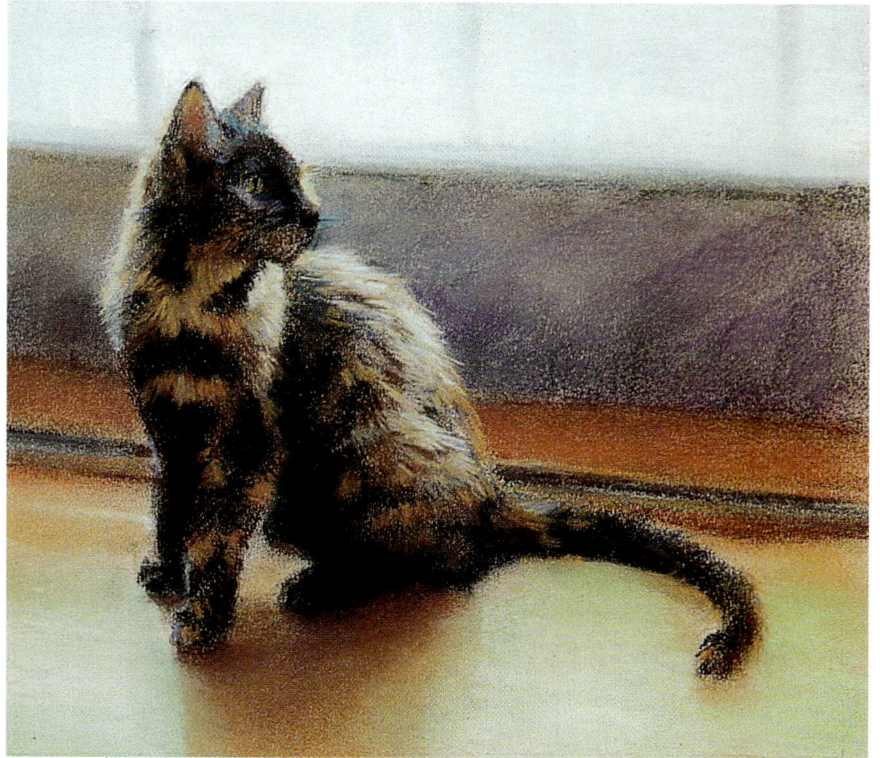

6 To complete the painting, I lighten the window with white to create more contrast and make it appear as if the light were shining through it. Then I add a little phthalo blue 10 to the sunlit areas of the floor, and I highlight the fur with yellow ochre 10 and phthalo blue 10.

4 I lighten the window with viridian green 9 and darken the wall with purple 3 and blue-gray 7. Then I add vermilion 3 and olive green 3 to the molding. For the dark accents in the shadowed fur, I add unblended strokes of carmine brown 3 and bistre 3. Next I add more detail with English red 3. I indicate the reflected light on the muzzle with cobalt blue 5 and use scarlet for the light shining through the ear. Then I add a little crimson 5 to add depth to the corner of the eye.

5 Now I decide to shorten the muzzle, using Mars violet 5 to paint the background into the nose a bit to define its shape. Then I go over the dark patches of fur with black, particularly in the tail. I use light English red 9 and cobalt blue 9 for details in the light areas, and I add thin strokes of cobalt blue 9 that trail off into the background to create the illusion of backlit fur. Then I paint into the edge of the tail with the floor color (gold ochre 5 and phthalo green 8).

Capturing a Likeness

As an artist, being able to create a recognizable portrait of a person is an extremely satisfying experience. Although it may seem challenging at first, painting a portrait is similar to painting an animal, landscape, or any other subject; look for the basic shapes and contours, and paint what you see. The key to portraiture is noticing the subtle differences in the features of each individual, such as a small nose, thin lips, or a high forehead, and making sure they're in the correct place and proportion. So when painting a live model—or from a photograph—the first and most important thing I do is define my subject's main features, beginning with the general outline of the head. For this portrait of Bethany, I first sketched the loose contours of her face and hair, and then I focused on her features and what makes each unique, carefully observing and copying the shapes and measuring the distances between them. (See the box on page 19.) Remember: As long as you draw what you *really* see (and not what you *expect* to see), your portrait will look like your model.

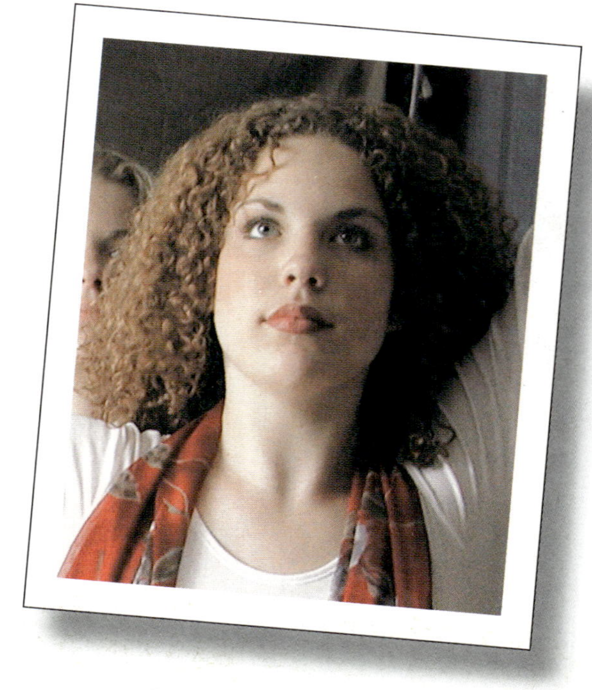

▶ **FOCUSING ON FEATURES**
I want to capture Bethany's calm determined gaze in my portrait, so I will focus on carefully defining the features of her face that contribute to that feeling. I pay close attention to rendering her wide eyes, set lips, and outstretched neck.

1 I begin my portrait of Bethany by working a light cool tone into the tooth of the paper with the side of my hand, painting around the area where her face and neck will be. I want to enhance her beautiful red hair and skin tones, so I use an extremely thin blend of permanent red dark 8 and phthalo green 8. Then, with vine charcoal, I establish the general size of her head and the placement of her features, as described in the box on page 19. I also place a few strokes of ultramarine blue 3 in the background and lightly blend them with a paper towel.

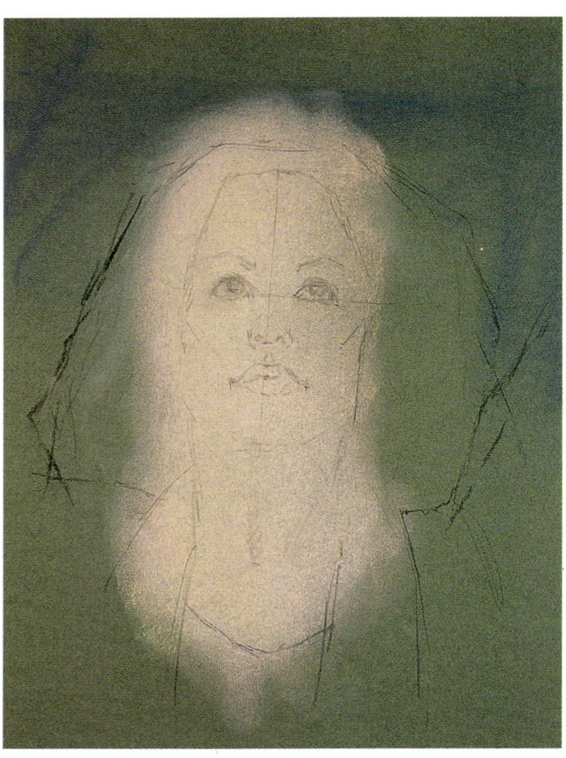

2 I start by establishing all the "extremes" of value, color, and definition (sharpness). I paint the darkest dark first—the black shadows in her hair—after wiping off some of the green base tone with a paper towel. Then I paint over the black with a little denatured alcohol and a brush to saturate the paper so none of the white paper shows through. Now I establish the lightest light—the white of Bethany's blouse—with blue-gray 9 and the most intense color—the red of her scarf—with scarlet 5. Next I determine that the sharpest edge is her right cheek; all other edges will be softer than this one. Now that the extremes are in place, I can compare every other element of the painting to them as I work.

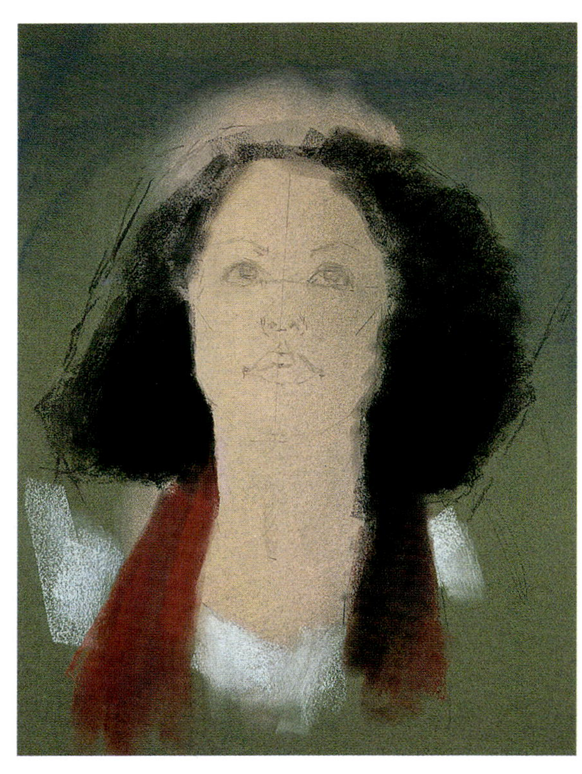

3 Next I paint in the warm shadow patterns. For the shadow on the side of her face and under her chin, I use primarily Indian red 3, with a little olive green 3 to cool it slightly. I paint the darks under her upper eyelids with Indian red 3 with a little black. I use vermilion 3 for her nostrils, madder lake deep 5 for her lips, and alizarin crimson 3 for the dark corner of her mouth. I establish the pupils of her eyes with black, and place some olive green 3 to indicate the irises. I'm not concerned with details at this point, only with the large shapes and colors.

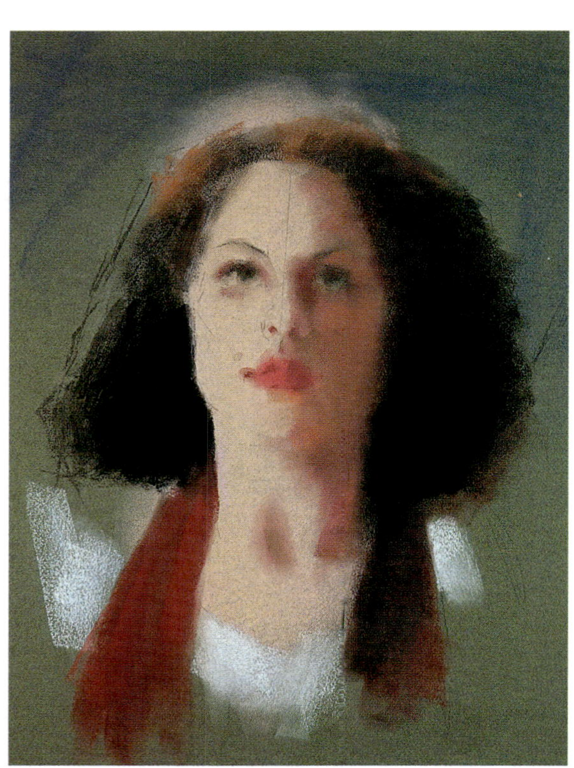

4 Here I block in more of the background tones with a deep gray-green. Then I paint the cool color of the "white" in her left eye and the shadows on her blouse with blue-gray 3. Next I darken her upper eyelashes with black and add some strokes of burnt sienna 5 for the dark red of her hair. I place madder lake deep 3 in the corners of her mouth and in her nostrils to darken them. As I paint, I blend every stroke with the side of my finger to keep the edges soft.

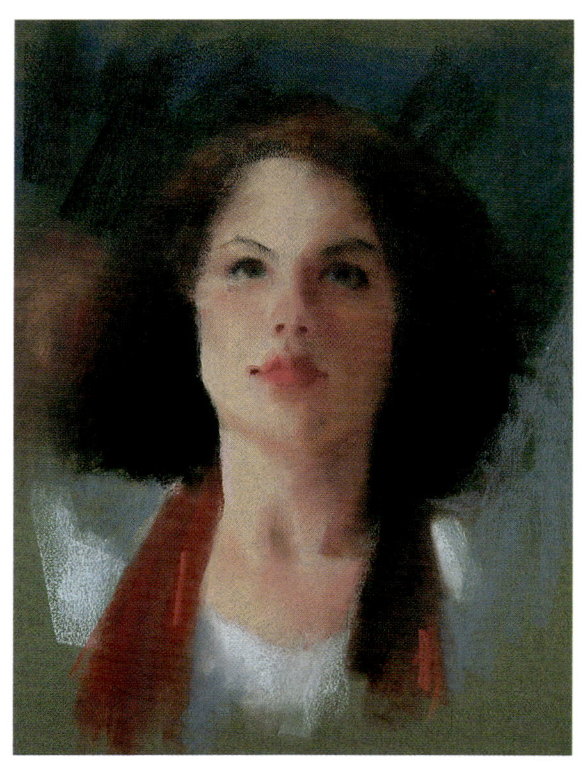

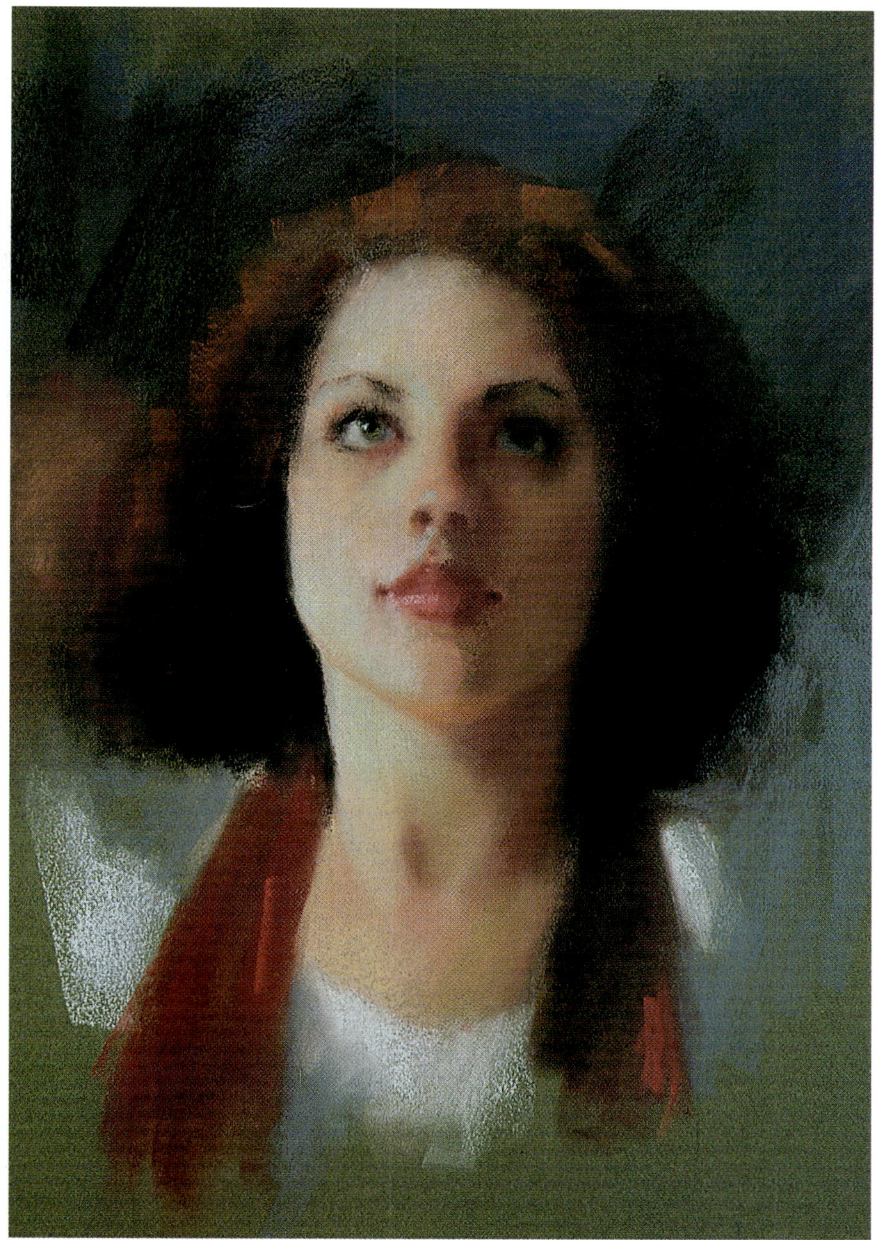

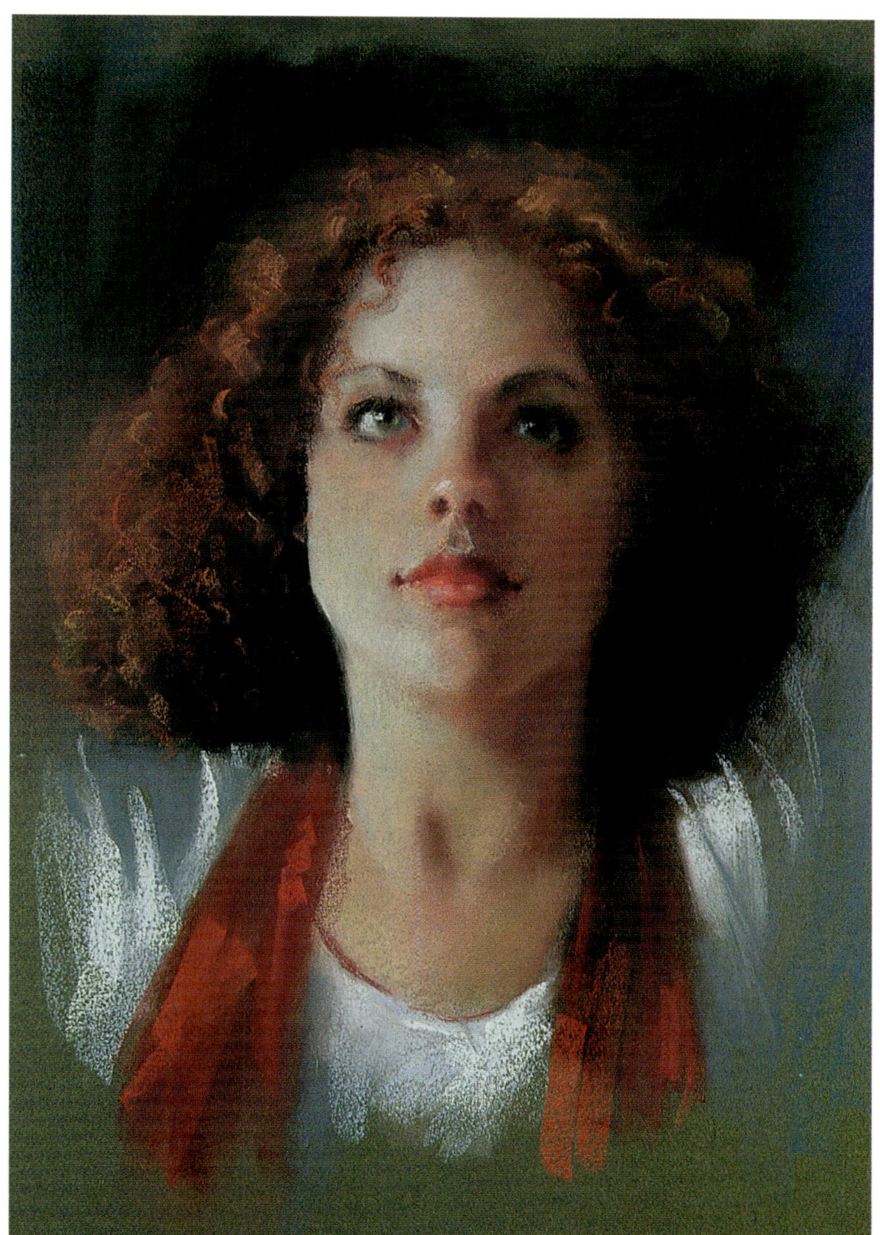

5 I use a few strokes of orange 3 to indicate the light areas of her hair and then move on to the light side of her face. I apply layers of permanent red deep 8 and phthalo green 8, blending well in the light areas. For the highlight on the right side of her nose, I use cobalt blue 8 and permanent red deep 9. Then I add some more darks (burnt umber 3 and alizarin crimson 3) to her eyelashes. I use two different values for the "whites" of her right eye: On the light side of the eye, I use blue-gray 7; on the shadow side, I use blue-gray 5 and 3. Note that the edges in eyes (the iris, the lashes, the border of the "whites") are all very soft; the only sharp stroke in the eye is the highlight of cobalt blue 9. Opposite the highlight, I place some olive green 5 on the iris. Then I use carmine 7 for the midtone on the front plane of the nose and chrome green 8 for the highlight. I darken her upper lip with Indian red 3 and vermilion 3, and use carmine 7 for the highlight on her lower lip.

6 Now I paint the light masses of the hair with broad strokes of scarlet 5, permanent red deep 5, and madder lake deep 5. I add touches of cobalt blue 7 to the light areas of her skin and lighten the highlight on the side of her nose with phthalo blue 9. I add a highlight on her left eye with blue-gray 5. Then I paint the highlight on her lower lip with red-violet 5; for the highlight above her lip, I use phthalo green 8. I add more darks to the background with black-green 3. Then I draw in a few light strokes to represent individual curls in her hair. I add the curl on her forehead with Indian red 3 and burnt sienna 5, but I don't blend these strokes excessively. I also add some olive green 5 to her hair to give it some variety and contrast. Finally I place a few bold strokes of permanent red light 5 in her scarf, and then I use Indian red 3 to indicate the cast shadows on the edges of her blouse and scarf.

Measuring for Accuracy

For portraiture, an accurate drawing will automatically produce a likeness. And accuracy is really nothing more than careful measurement. At the beginning stages of my drawing, I'm not concerned with details—I just want the placement of the features to be correct. First I establish a basic unit of measurement (usually the width of one of the model's eyes). Then I use this unit to measure and mark the distances between each facial landmark. (See photo and caption at right.) I also consider the angles between the features; the easiest way to do this is to compare my model's face to the face of a clock. I use a pencil to represent the hands of the clock, which helps me determine the angle at which to place the features. (For example, I might decide the eyes should be placed at 10:00 and 2:00.) Once I'm confident my measurements are correct, I look carefully to see what is unique about each feature and draw their basic shapes. Then I step back, assess my work from a distance or in a mirror (a good way to test whether the features are symmetrical), and make any necessary corrections. These measurements may seem time-consuming, but achieving a good likeness is worth the extra effort.

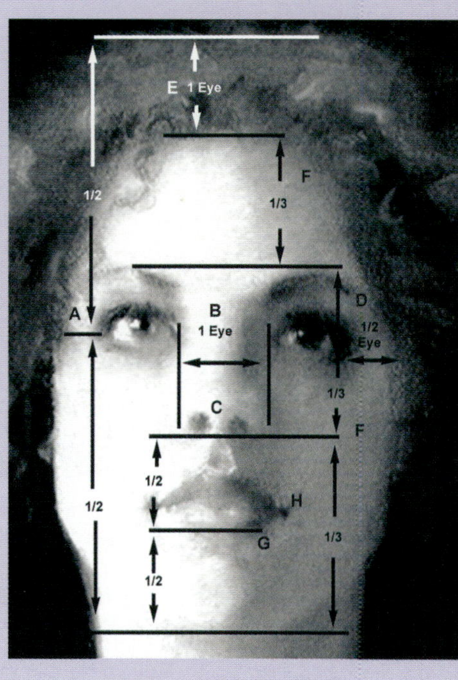

CHOOSING A GOOD UNIT OF MEASUREMENT In this example, I use the model's right eye as a unit of measurement. As you can see in the diagram at left, I measure all the other facial proportions based on one "eyewidth." For example, the highest part of her eyebrow is one eye-width above her lower eyelid. I also look at general proportions—the distance from the top of her eyebrows to her hairline is a little bit less than the distance from the base of her nose to the top of her eyebrows. Angles are also important; the pupil of her right eye is at about 9:30 in relation to the inner corner of her eye.

Using Colored Paper

When you work on colored paper, the support becomes an integral part of the painting, instead of just a surface to be covered with pastel. Unless the color is applied very heavily, the pigment sits on top of the raised grain, allowing the paper to show through the strokes. Therefore the paper you choose can either set the overall tone for the painting—light, medium, or dark—or provide a warm or cool color contrast. The color of the paper can also be used to either add weight and depth to your painting, stand in for a dominant color, harmonize with the palette, or provide a contrasting tone. You can also choose a colored ground that will serve as a middle value and remain uncovered, so that all you need to paint are the light and dark values. For this painting of Katherine, I chose a warm burgundy paper as the base color to complement and mingle with the warm reds and yellows in the shadows, beautifully offsetting the cool, reflected light on Katherine's face. And by letting the paper stand in for some of the color, I was able to keep the background loosely painted, maintaining the focus on my subject.

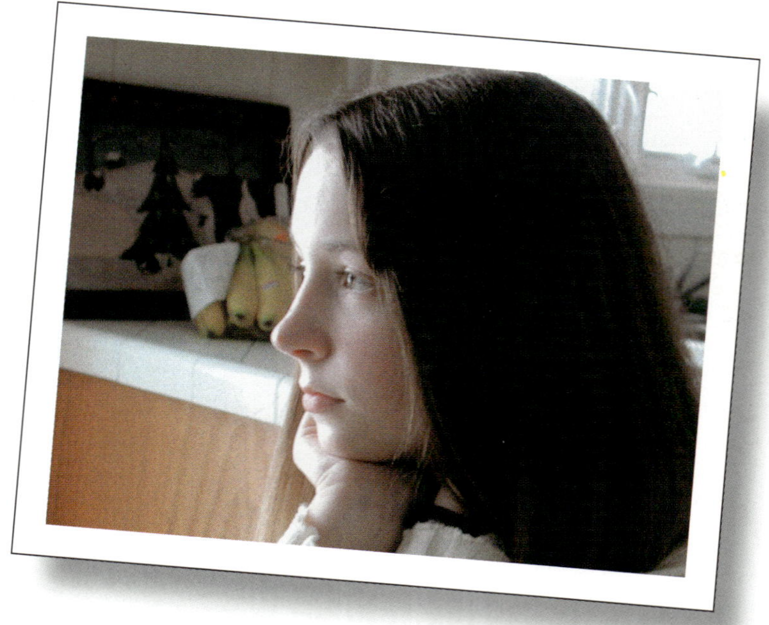

CANDID PHOTOS Normally it's best to paint from life; our eyes see colors, values, and edges much more accurately than a photo can reproduce them. But a camera can be useful for capturing fleeting expressions. I was painting an oil portrait of Katherine when I caught her gazing wistfully out the window on a break, lost in thought. So I grabbed my digital camera and snapped this photo.

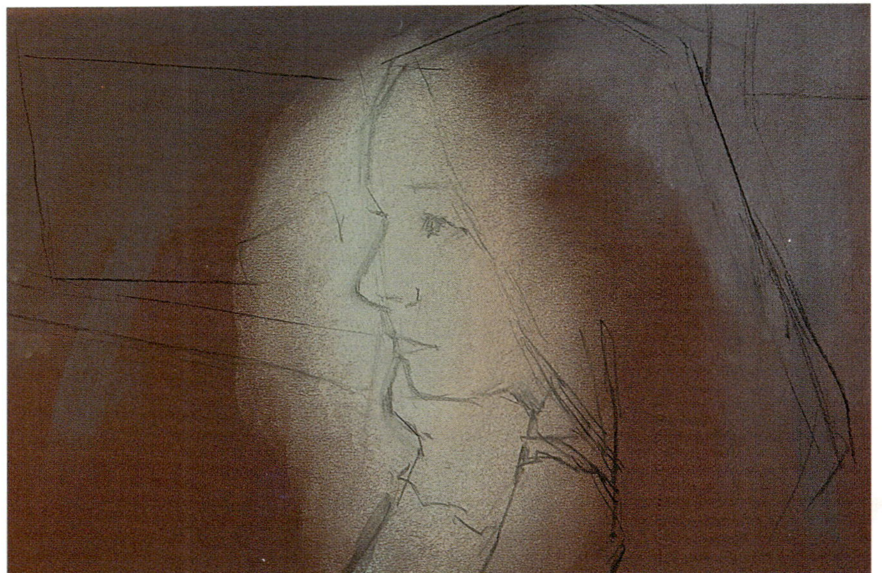

1 I first apply a thin, light base tone of alizarin crimson 8 with a layer of phthalo green 8 around the area where I will place the face. I blend the color with circular movements and work it into the tooth of the paper with the side of my hand. Then, using soft vine charcoal, I draw in the main features on her face. This is the most important step in capturing a likeness, but is also the most mechanical. I start by defining the top and bottom of the head and the general profile. I go from one facial landmark to the next, comparing each to the previous feature. (See pages 18 and 19.)

2 Next I establish the darkest dark (the shadow areas of her hair and her sweater). I use a soft paper towel to wipe off the light pastel where her hair will be, and then I cover the area with black. I dip a soft brush dipped in some denatured alcohol and paint the dark pigment thoroughly into the tooth of the paper. Then I place a swatch of ultramarine blue where the highlight in her hair will be. I also establish some of the background colors with olive green 5 and blue-gray 5. I like to work on the background and foreground of a painting at the same time—this way the whole piece has a sense of color harmony.

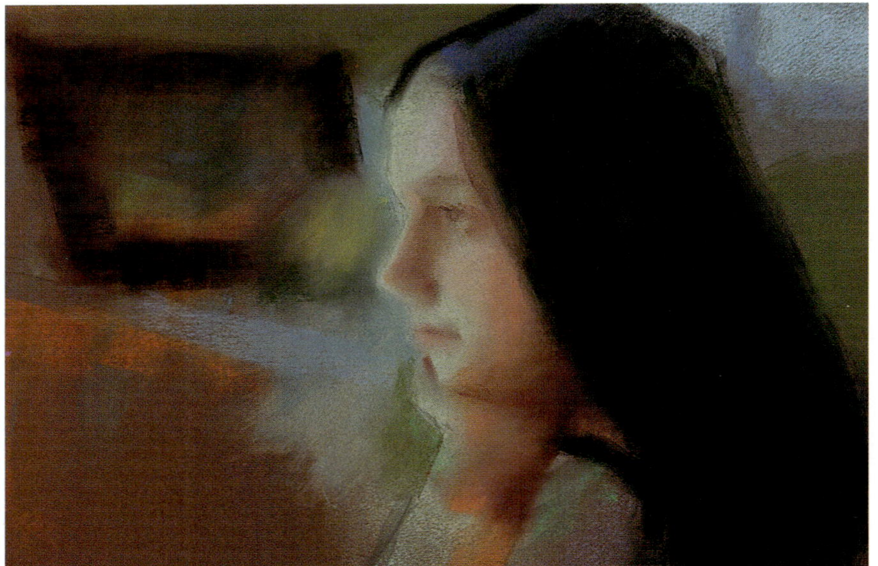

3 Now I establish the shadow pattern on her face, keeping in mind that the cool light produces warm shadows. I use Indian red 3 for the deepest shadows under her chin and a 5 value for the lighter shadows on the side of her nose and around her eye. For the *halftone* (middle value) on the side of her cheek, I use carmine 8, blending all the colors with my fingers to produce a very soft, even tone. Then I add a few strokes of dark vermilion to indicate some of the deeper shadow in her hair. I also block in the brown rectangular shape on the left side of the picture with burnt umber 3. Then I suggest the window with mouse gray 7 and cobalt blue 7, and I add warm orange strokes of burnt sienna 5 to the foreground.

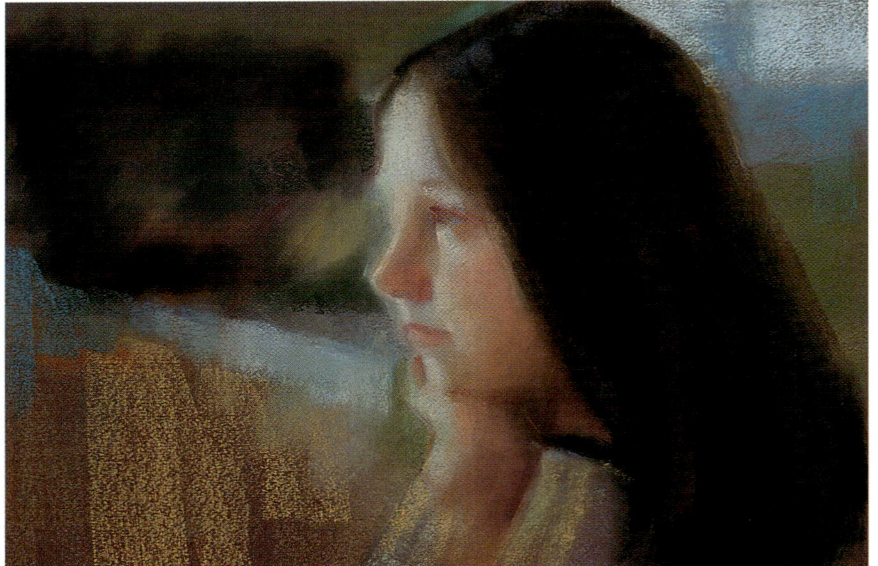

4 I work on the halftones by applying alternating layers of carmine red 7 and olive green 8. Then, on the lower third of her face, I use the same colors in a 5 value (but with a little more emphasis on the green). Here I use the side of my finger to wipe and blend virtually every stroke, as I want the skin to appear very smooth. Next I cool the shadow under her chin with olive green 3, and then I use Indian red 5 for the shadows on her upper lip and in the corner of her eye. I paint the shadowed sleeve of her left arm with mouse gray 5 and blue-violet 5, adding gold ochre 7 and phthalo green 7 for the lighter areas. Then I begin to work burnt umber 3 into her hair to give it a more brownish tone, and I lighten the highlight on her hair with cobalt blue 7.

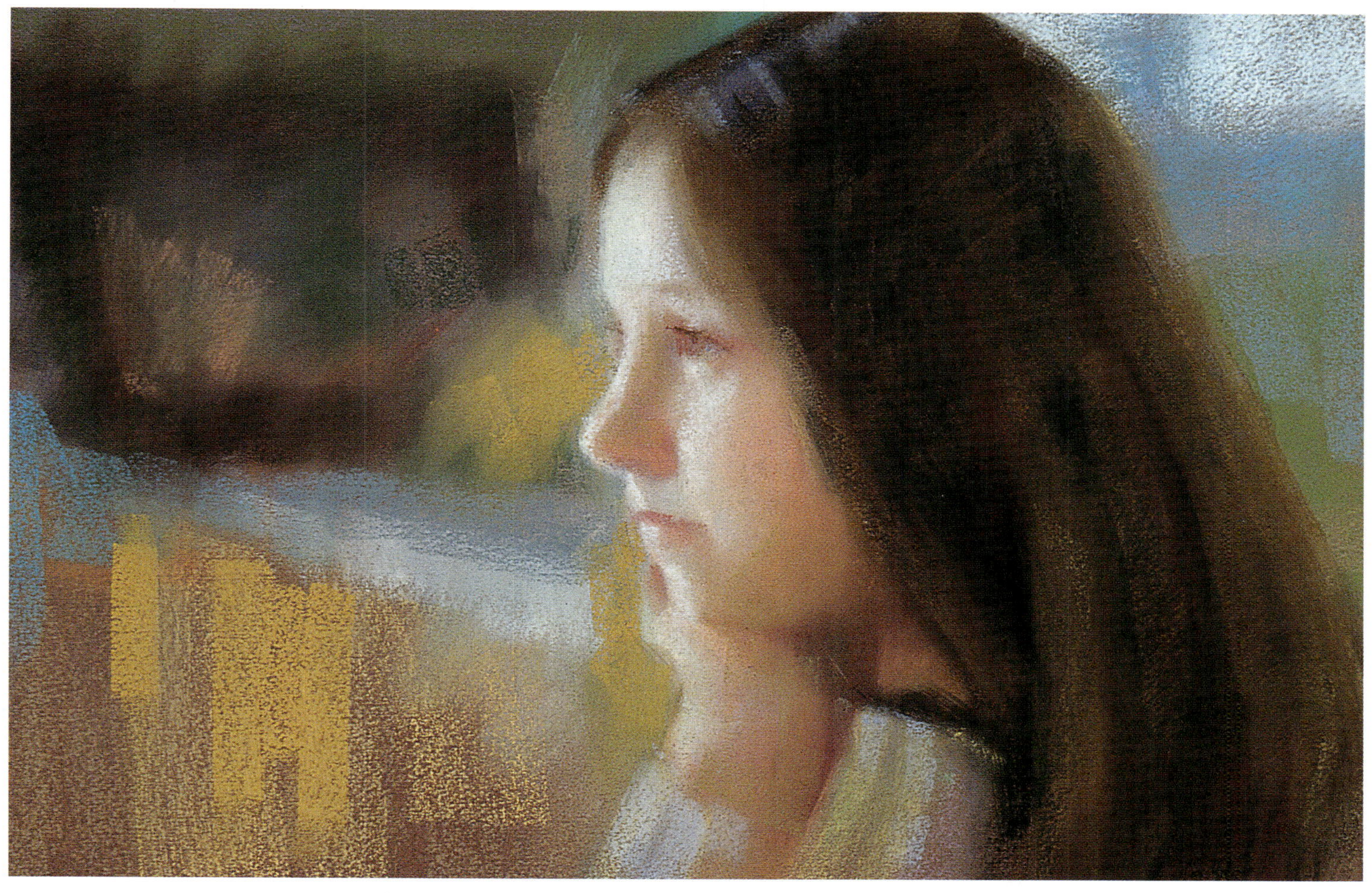

5 Next I work on the light areas of her face. I use thin layers of permanent red 9 and phthalo blue 9 for the lights in her forehead and permanent red 8 and cobalt blue 8 for the lights in the middle of her face. I add the lights in the lower third of her face with permanent red 8 and chrome green 8. Then I darken the shadow of the upper eyelid with a little black; I also touch black in the center of the eye to indicate the pupil. I work more colors into the background, with strokes of gold ochre 3, carmine 3, and olive green 5. I blend these strokes slightly with the side of my finger.

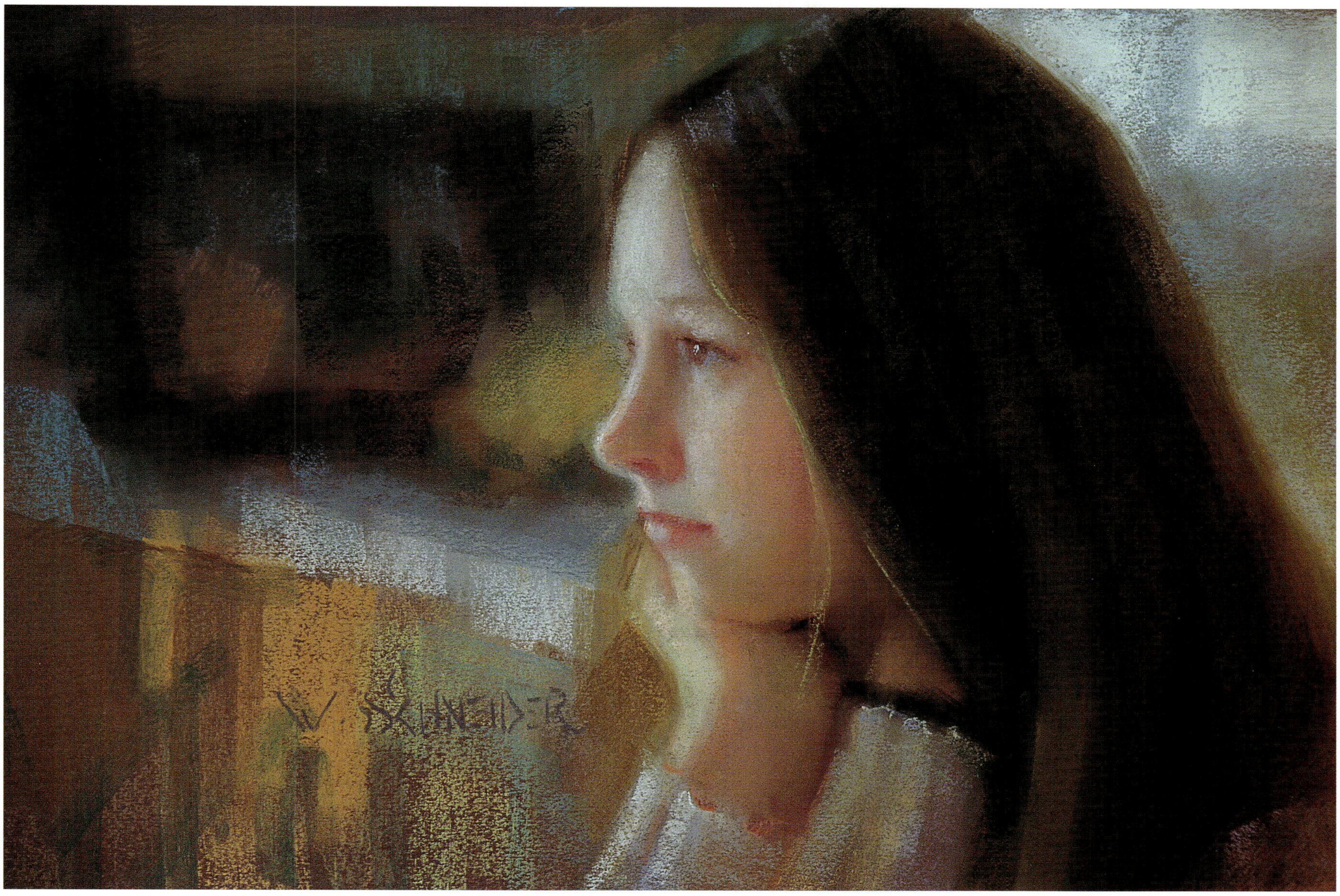

6 To finish, I use burgundy 2 to indicate the deepest dark tones under her chin and in the corner of her mouth; then I place umber 2 in some of the recesses of her hair. I add the highlight in her eye with a single dash of turquoise blue 10. Opposite and below the highlight, I place a touch of chrome green 5. I blend in a stroke of chrome green 10 for the highlight on her nose (skin is less reflective than the moist surface of the eye). I sharpen the edge of the sweater on her left sleeve with blue-gray 5. Then I blend strokes of orange 8 and olive green 8 to show where the light catches a few strands of hair. Finally I add a red-violet deep 7 highlight on her lower lip and then step back to check my work. I'm pleased with the painting, and I sign my name.

Developing the Human Form

Throughout the ages, artists have been captivated by the beauty of the human form. And learning to paint the human figure is just a matter of seeing the basic shapes and how these shapes flow together into a form. Think of the body as composed of a series of cylinders—or rounded oblongs—and the head as a sphere. After drawing the basic shapes, all you need to do is develop these shapes into solid forms with varying values, shadows, and highlights. But even before you start sketching the shapes, it's a good idea to look at your subject and determine the *line of action*—an imaginary line (or lines) that establishes the extent and direction of the pose. It can be as simple as the curve in the back of this seated figure or as complex as the angled limbs of an athlete in motion. The important thing is to make sure that all the parts of the body conform to the line of action. For example, in this woman's graceful pose, you can see that the curve of her body extends from her head through her leg, which is then counterbalanced by her supporting right arm.

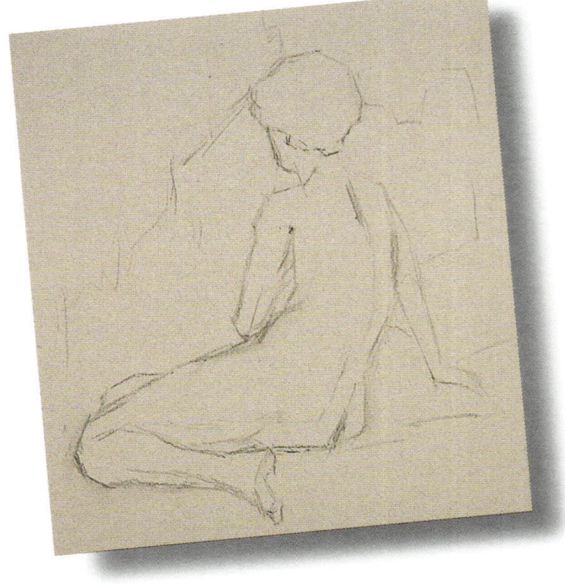

◄ **ESTABLISHING THE POSE**
First I sketch the outline of the figure using vine charcoal. At this point, all I want is the overall gesture of the pose and the line of action. I also indicate where I will block in some background around the figure.

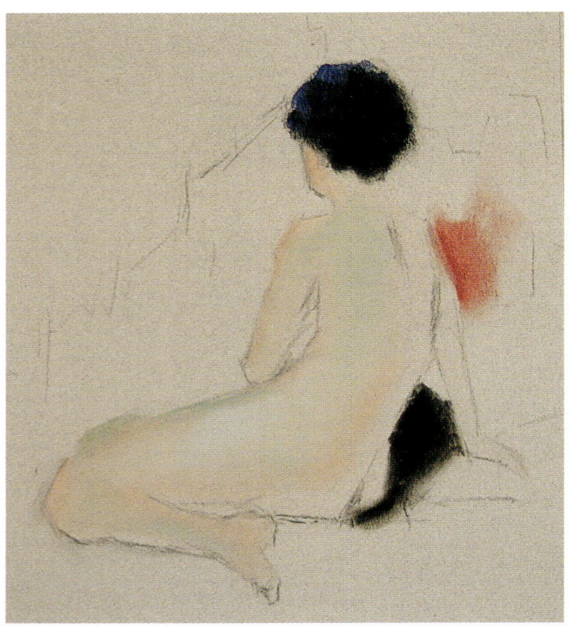

1 As usual, I first place my extremes so that I have a standard of comparison for succeeding values, colors, and strokes. I paint the lightest light—the cool flesh tones of her hip and upper leg—with permanent red deep 8 and phthalo green 8 and rub them into the tooth of the paper with my hand. The darkest dark is the black of her hair and the shadow to the right. To ensure that none of the paper shows through here, I blend the black into the paper with a light wash of denatured alcohol. Then I block in the area of most intense color: the vermilion red to the right of her shoulder.

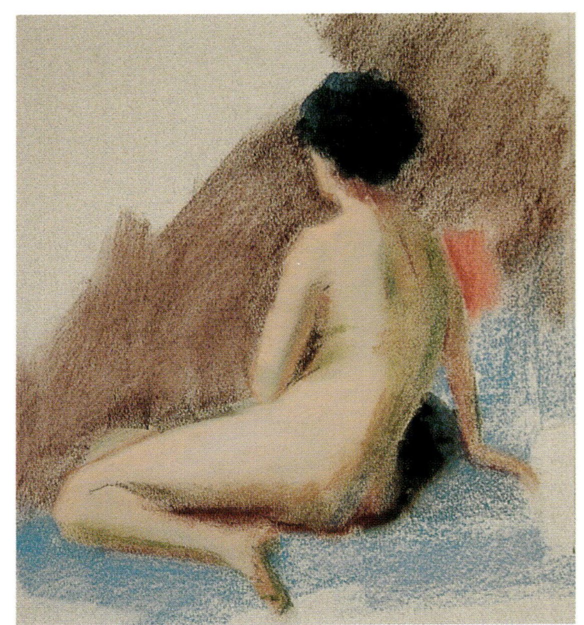

2 Next I paint the shadows on the figure with olive green 3 and 5 and caput mortuum red 7. I use umber 3 for the shadow core (the darkest part of the shadow, which normally lies between the halftone and the reflected light). Then I paint some of the background colors to set off the figure from the light paper. I use burnt sienna 3 for the darkest areas in front of and to the right of the figure. Then I wipe it with a paper towel to blend the strokes and to remove all but a thin layer of pastel. For the surface on which she is sitting (the drape), I use turquoise blue 5 and phthalo blue 3.

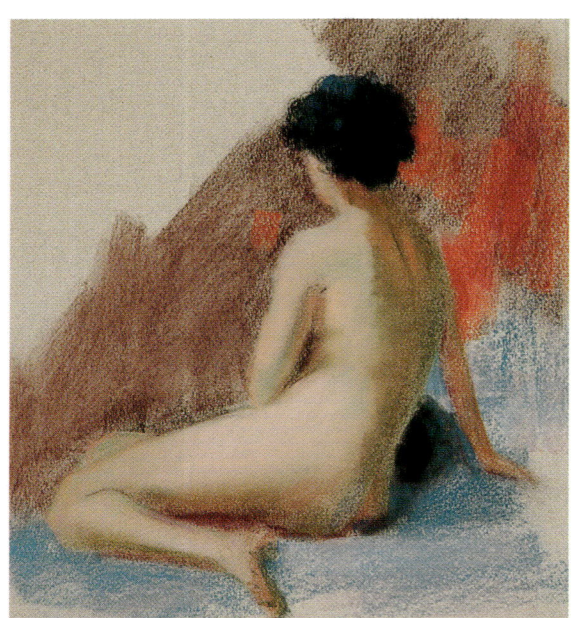

3 I want to contrast the smoothness of the flesh with the texture in the background, so I add a few bold, unblended strokes of permanent red 5 to the right of her head and above her left shoulder. Then I cool the edges of her leg with phthalo green 7. This helps create the illusion that the leg is turning away from the viewer. Next I lighten the highlight on the thigh with permanent red deep 9, cobalt blue 7, permanent rose 10, and gold ochre 9.

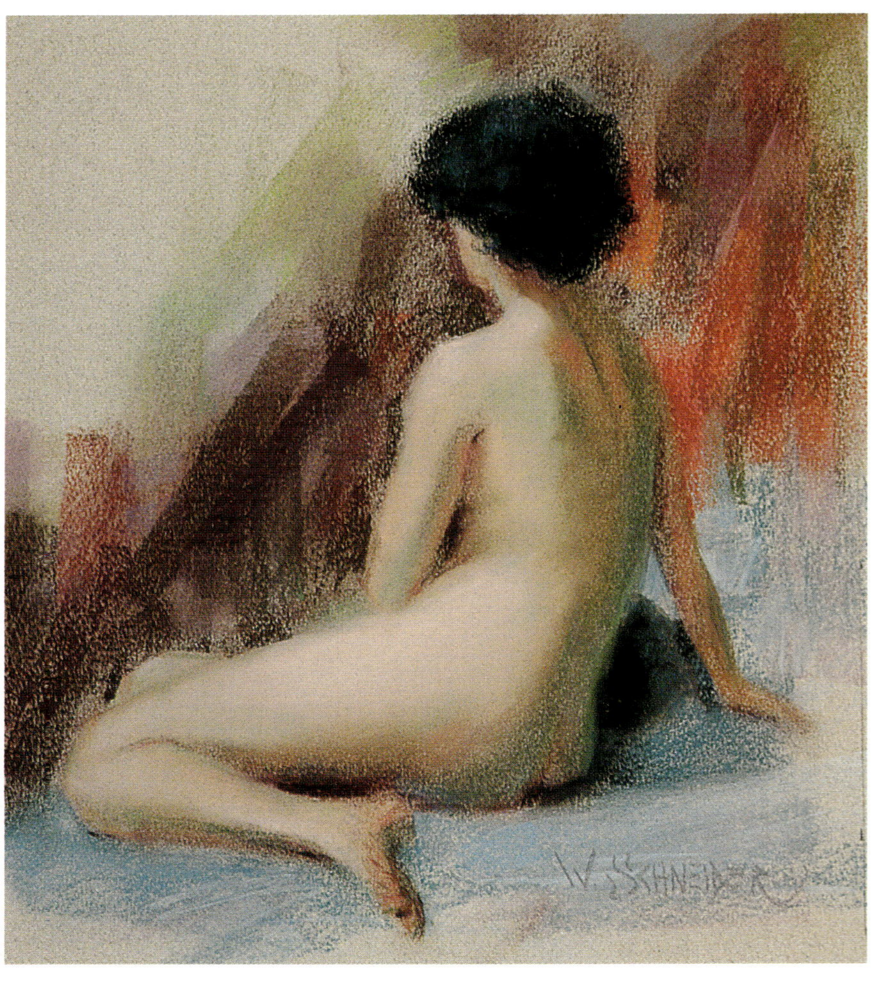

4 I sign my name with a light color that won't distract from the subject. But when I step back to look at the piece from a distance, I decide the curve of her body is a little too strong. I straighten her back by painting some of the background red into the edge of her shoulder and adding turquoise blue 5 to the space between her right arm and her back. Then I lighten her leg by adding pure white. As I paint the skin tones, I blend each stroke with a swipe of my finger, making sure to clean my finger on a paper towel between strokes. Next I enlarge the mass of hair a bit and add ultramarine blue 5 for the highlights. For the reflected light on her buttocks, I use blue-green 5; for the reflected light on her arm, I use scarlet 5. Then I add a stroke of gold ochre 9 for the highlight on her left leg and burnt umber 3 to indicate the deep dark shadow above her calf.

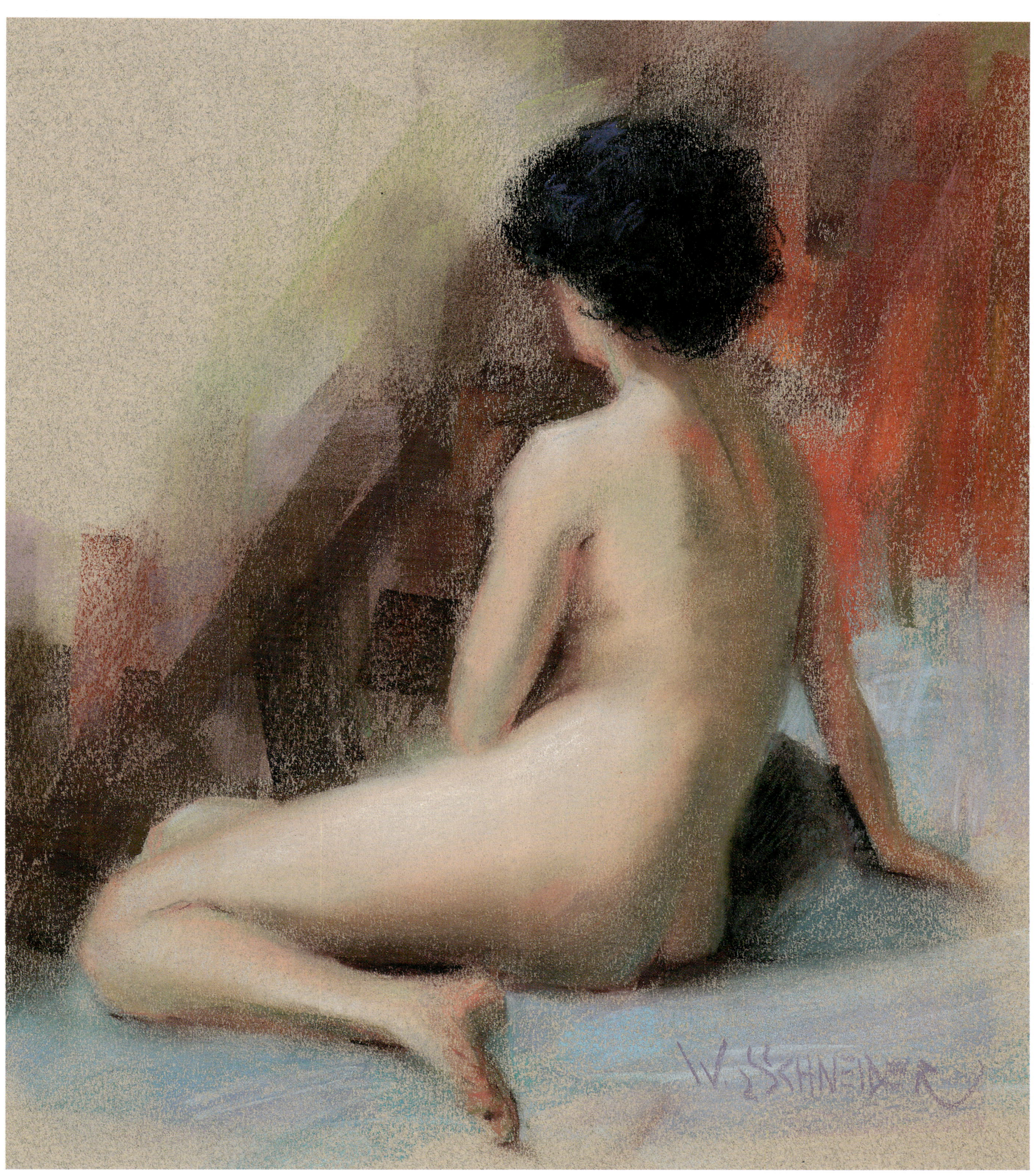

5 Now that I'm satisfied with the pose and the line of action, I complete the painting by adding a few more bold strokes of color to the background. Then I use bistre 3 to sharpen the upper edge of her thigh, the area around her knee, and the area around her chin. I also slightly sharpen the edges around her buttocks. Finally I add a few strokes of red-violet 7 to lighten the background on the far right. Now I step back again and assess the painting. I am satisfied that I have captured the pose accurately and have rendered the forms well without overworking the piece. Happy that I have also achieved a good balance between the figure and the background, I decide the piece is finished.

Depicting Flowers

Flowers are wonderful subjects for pastel paintings. They are not only easily accessible (you need only step out the door to find "models" for your work), they are also incredibly diverse. I am always intrigued by the different types of petal edges—from razor sharp to completely lost. (See page 6 for more on edges.) In fact, there are so many different varieties of flowers, with their myriad shapes and colors, that you can produce dozens of paintings without ever portraying the same flower twice. And although you can always paint a just a single blossom or two, a bouquet of several flowers offers the opportunity to use the brilliant pigments of pastel to their fullest. But choosing what flowers to include is just the first step; the next is to decide how to place them. When arranging a group of flowers, strive for an asymmetrical setup to add a sense of movement, as I have done with this composition. Fight the tendency to make all the flowers the same size, to space them regularly, and to place them in even rows. Your painting will be much more effective if the arrangement is dynamic and the blossoms aren't carbon copies of one another.

1 First I draw all the main shapes using vine charcoal on a dark-toned, sanded pastel board. To create a sense of movement, I place the center of interest (the second peony from the left) slightly off-center and position another blossom in front of the vase to draw in the viewer's eye. I also sketch in a vertical centerline for the vase and then measure how far the sides are away from that line. Then I establish my darkest values, using ivory black and carmine brown 2. Because this is a sanded support, I don't want to blend with my hands, so I work the colors into the support with a brush dampened in denatured alcohol.

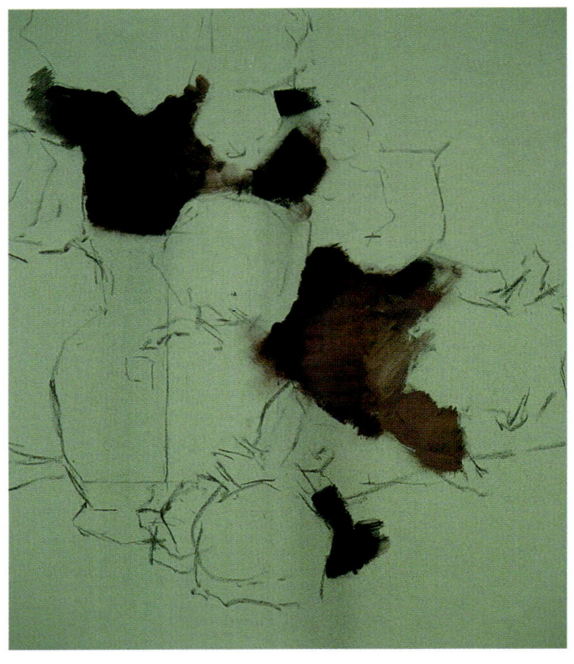

2 Next I use blue-gray 7 and lemon yellow 7 to establish the lightest light—the flower on the right. Then I apply madder lake deep 5—the most intense color—for the flower I've chosen as my center of interest. Next I paint in the background flowers with Indian red 5 and blue-gray 3, and I block in the tabletop with mouse gray 5. I use blue-violet 3 for the vase and blend the strokes with a paper stump and an occasional swipe of my fingers. At this point I've covered a lot of the board surface and established my extremes of value and color.

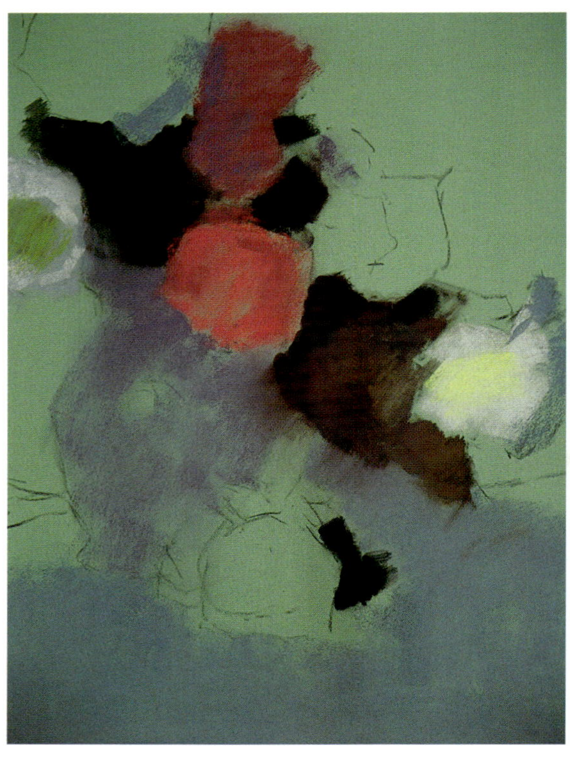

3 Next I fill in the background with gray-green 3 and indicate some of the leaves with olive green 3. I create the flowers on the table with madder lake deep 5, and I paint the bud on the right with Indian red 5. Then I add Indian red 3 to the vase and add blue-gray 5 to the middle white flower. Now the basic design of the arrangement becomes more apparent.

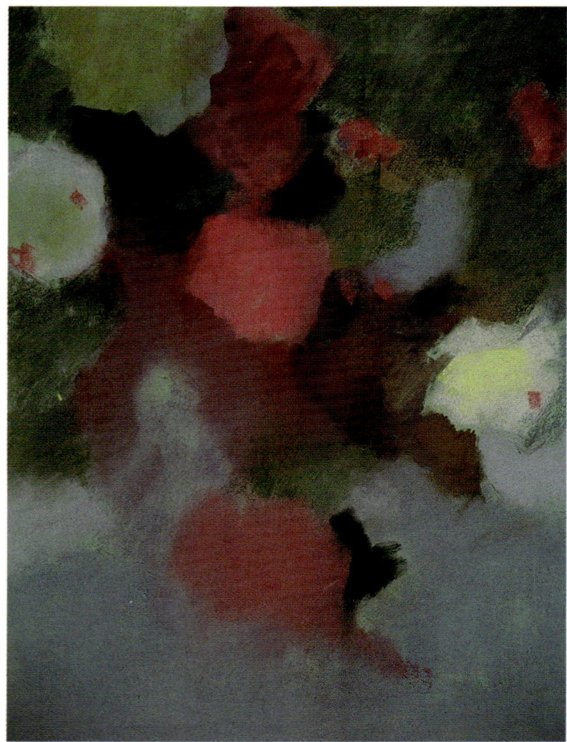

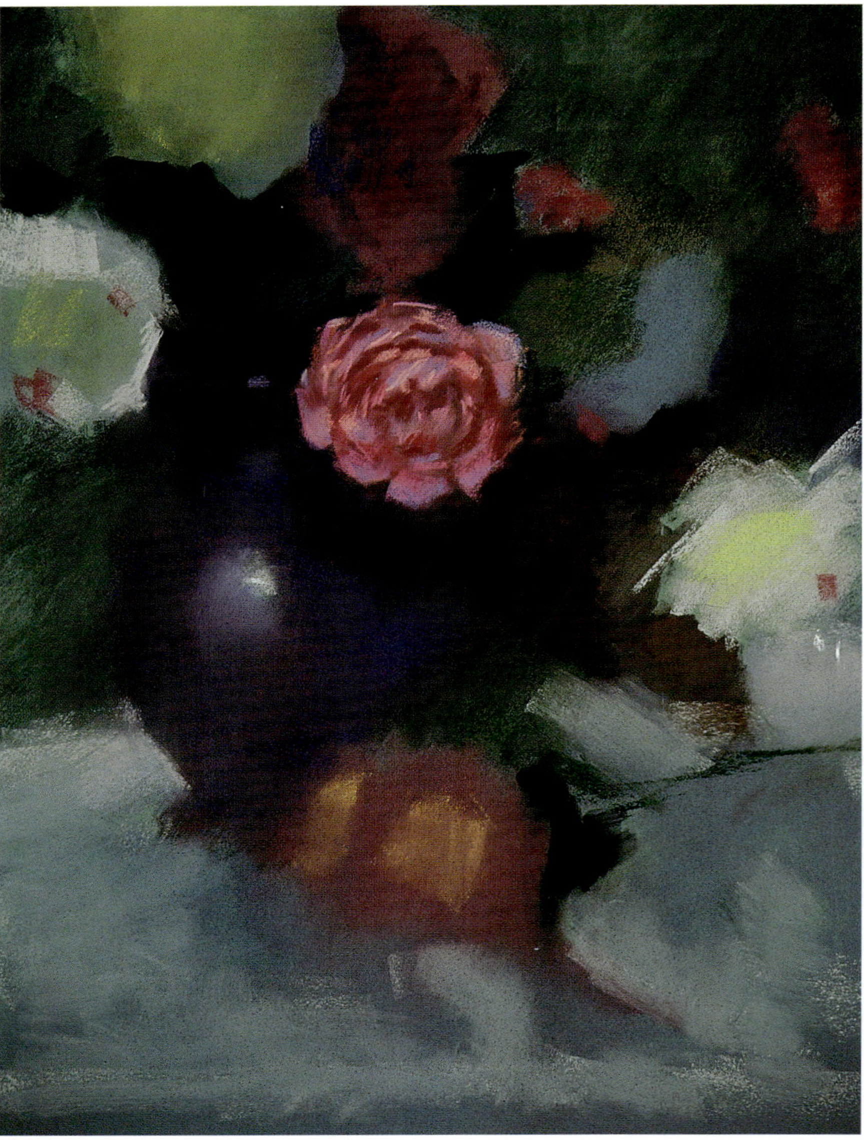

4 Now I paint around the center flower with cobalt violet 2 to define the petals. Then I use blue-violet 5, carmine 5 and 7, and permanent rose 7 for the lighter areas; for the deep recesses between the petals, I use burgundy 3. I paint a few strokes of gray 7 to show where the light is hitting the two white flowers, and then I draw the stems of the peonies on the table with blue-green 3, adding yellow 5 for the lighter petals. I paint the darker parts of the vase with cobalt violet 2 and use a little black to help define the area below the top rim. I indicate the main highlight by first creating a lighter area with blue-violet 5 and then adding a sharp (unblended) stroke of phthalo green 8. Then I sharpen the edge of the vase on the lower-left side with gray 5. Higher up on the vase, I intentionally blend the edges into the background; these lost edges convey the illusion that the object is turning away from the viewer.

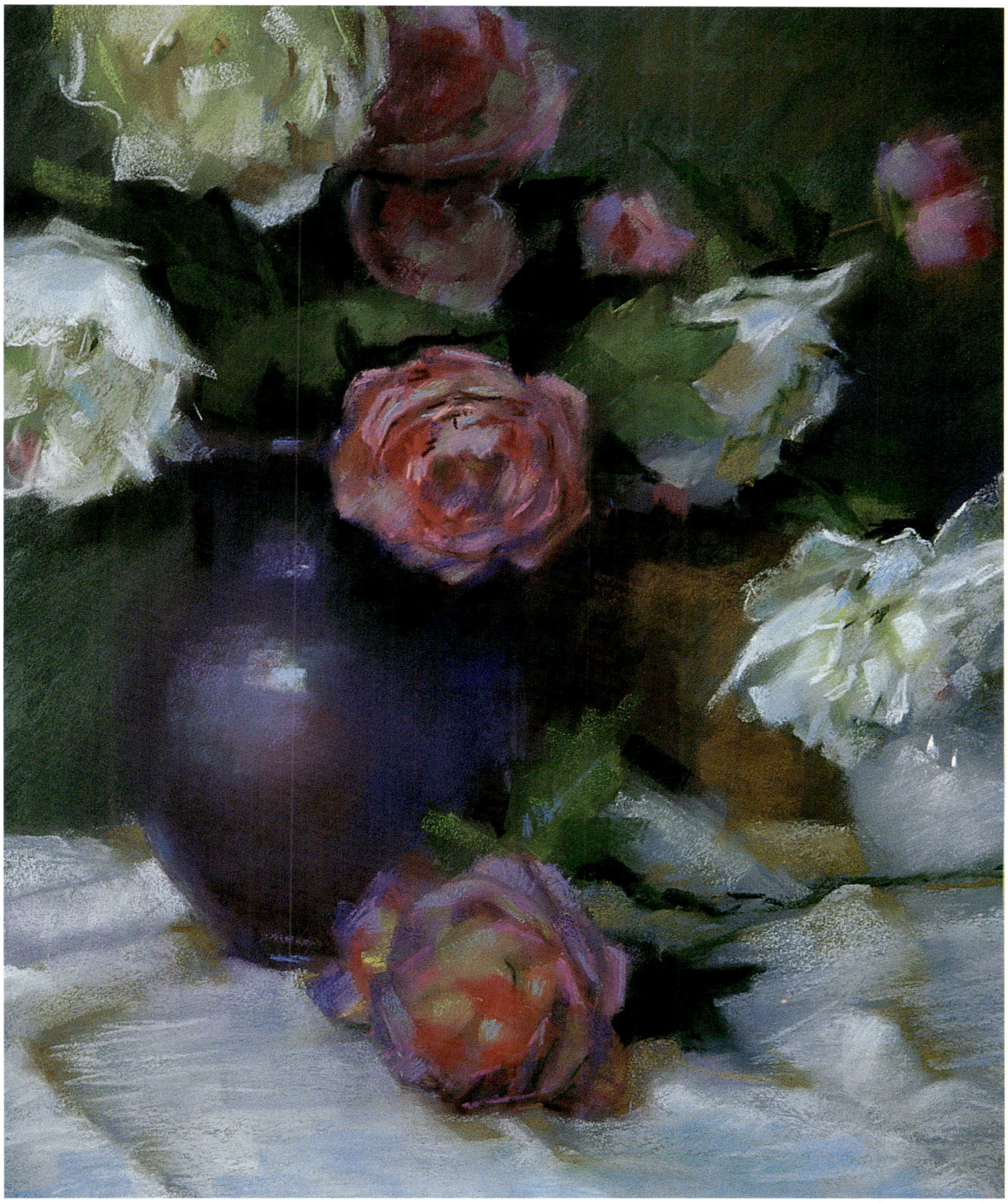

7 I decide that the center of interest is too light, so I darken it with permanent rose 5 and blue-violet 5. I also refine the outline of the petals to make them less regular. (I don't make up these shapes; I look closely at the actual flower.) Then I darken the vase with cobalt violet 2 and simplify the folds in the tablecloth with blue-gray 7 and 9. I use phthalo blue 10 to make the light at the edge of the table appear to come forward, and I define the outer petals of the three top white peonies with simple strokes of blue-gray 7. Finally I add a couple of small, sharp strokes of cobalt blue 9 to indicate the highlights at the neck of the vase.

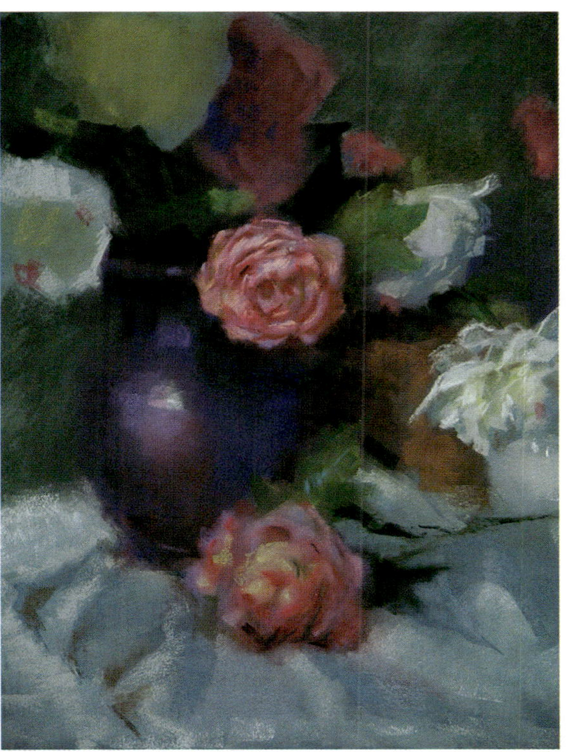

5 Now I add blue-gray 5 and 7 to the white flower on the lower right. I paint the dark recesses between the petals with blue-violet 3, olive green 5, and yellow ochre 3. Then I use Indian red 5, red-violet 7, and lemon yellow 5 for the pink flowers lying on the table and burgundy 3 for the dark shadows. I paint the leaves with olive green 5, and I highlight the lower peonies' leaves with turquoise 7. At this stage, I blend virtually every stroke to keep the edges soft.

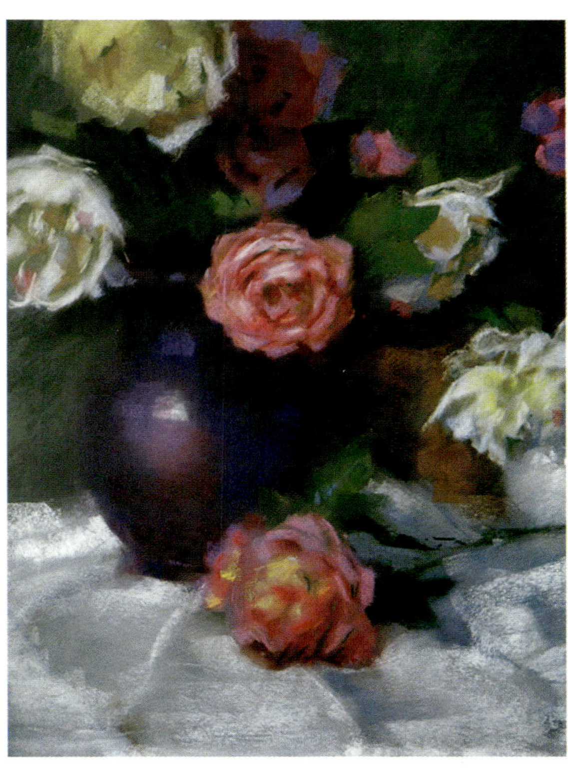

6 For the lights on the distant pink flower and buds, I add blue-violet 5. Then I refine the light peony at the top left with simple strokes of blue-gray 5 and 7 and indicate the recesses with yellow ochre 3. As I move away from the center of interest, I add less detail, which reflects the way we see. When we look directly at an object, we see sharp edges and a wealth of detail, whereas objects in our peripheral vision appear less sharply defined. (Of course, if we turn our gaze to them, then they become clearer.)

Detecting Color in White

Snow is a joy to paint! Like any white object, it has a wonderfully reflective surface, so it is anything but pure white. Instead it mirrors the colors of the sky and the other elements around it. And I love the way the interlocking light and dark shapes in a snowy winter landscape create visually interesting patterns, while the roughness of the terrain adds even more variations in color temperature and value. In this wintry scene, notice that the only true white areas are the lightest highlights, where the sun hits the snow directly. And rather than making my shadow areas a flat gray, I fill them with touches of the cool blues and greens reflected from the sky and the surrounding trees and bushes. Also keep in mind that reflected colors don't have to be dramatic to make an impact; subtle variations can be just as effective, as you can see in this painting of snow-capped trees on a frosty winter morning.

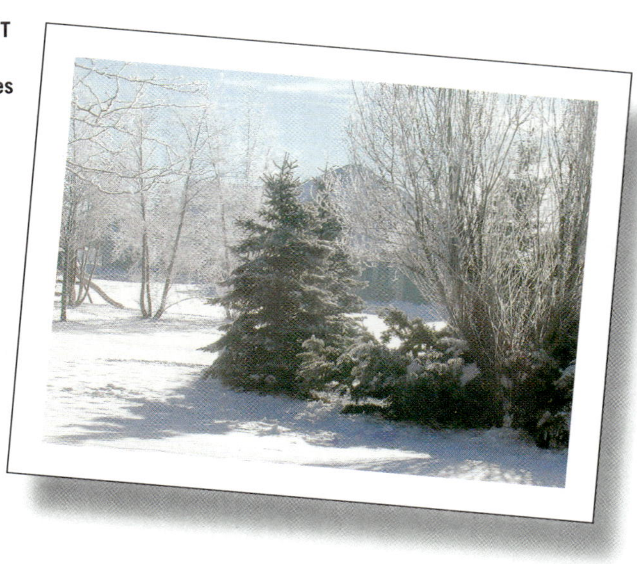

▶ **SIMPLIFYING A SUBJECT**
This photo shows all the intricate details of the trees in this scene, but notice that I simplified them greatly in my painting. Remember that you don't have to render every branch or every leaf to make a believable tree; just paint the shapes you see, and the viewer's eye will fill in the details.

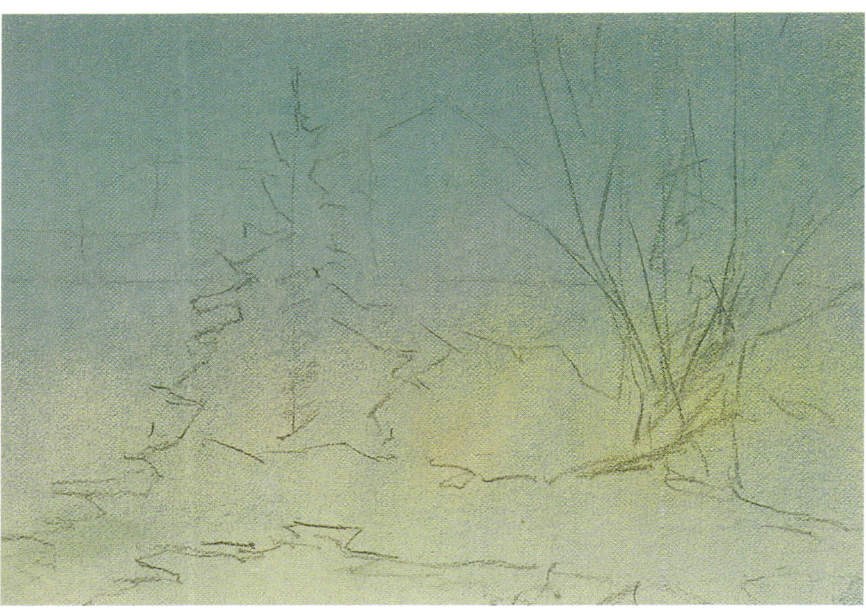

1 I want the dominant color of this piece to be blue-green to help evoke the cold feeling of this frigid winter day. So I begin by toning the sky with blue-green 7, deep yellow 9, red-violet 9, and phthalo green 8, making the top part of the paper a little darker than the lower part. Then I draw in the main shapes with vine charcoal, indicating where I want the dark shapes to be sandwiched between lights. Now I'm ready to establish the darkest darks in the scene.

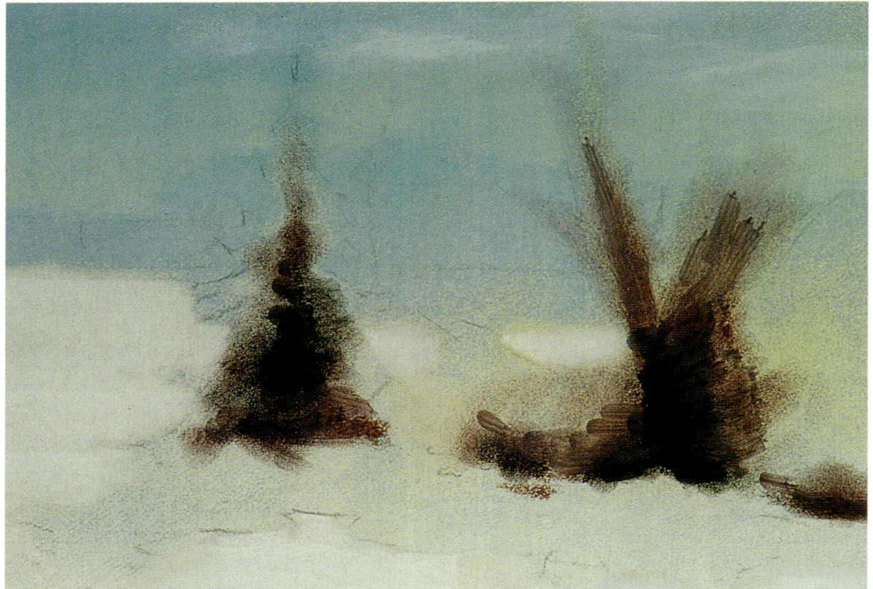

2 I paint the trees with a warm mixture of vermilion 3 and ivory black. Then I brush a denatured alcohol wash over the area to make sure none of the light paper shows through. Next I indicate the background with turquoise blue 5 and the wispy clouds with blue-gray 8. I then create the lightest light in the snow with deep yellow 9 and 12 and scarlet 10. These colors are almost white, but they maintain a bit of warmth that helps to portray the bright sunlit snow.

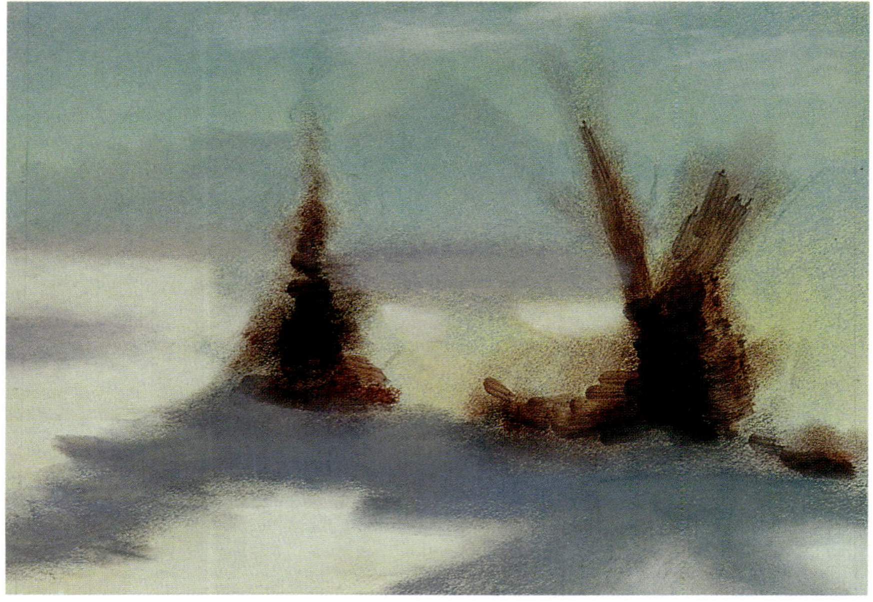

3 Because the snow reflects the blue sky, there is a cool tone to the shadows in this piece. Here I use blue-gray 5, mouse gray 7, and blue-violet 3 and 5 to indicate the shadows that mirror the trees and bushes. I make the more distant shadows a little lighter and more violet in tone, and then I blend all the shadows with the side of my hand.

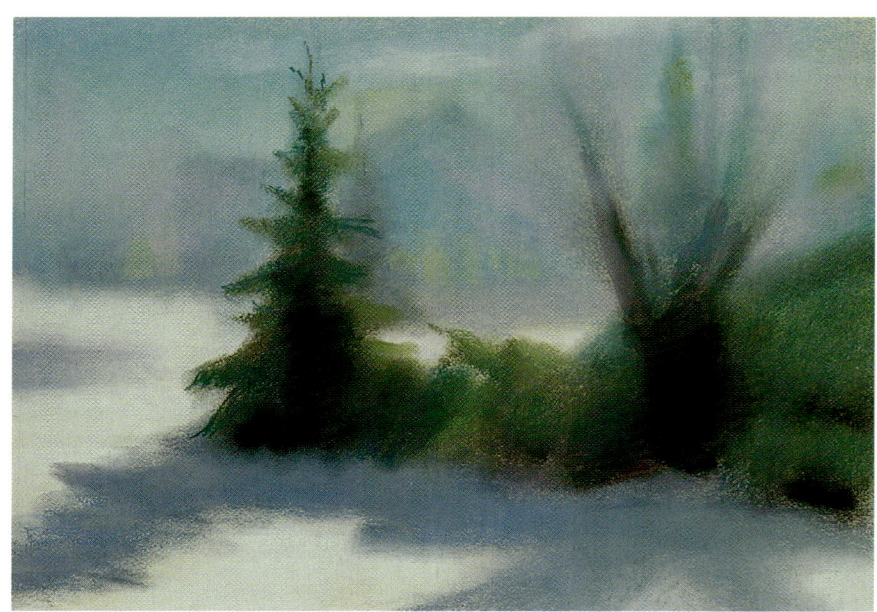

4 Now I block in the pine trees. I place black and scarlet 3 for the shadowed branches and ultramarine blue 3 near the deepest darks. For the rest of the pine trees, I use a mix of blue-green 3 and olive green 3. Because the trees are backlit, there are very few variations in value. However I paint some of the places where light shines through the branches with olive green 5.

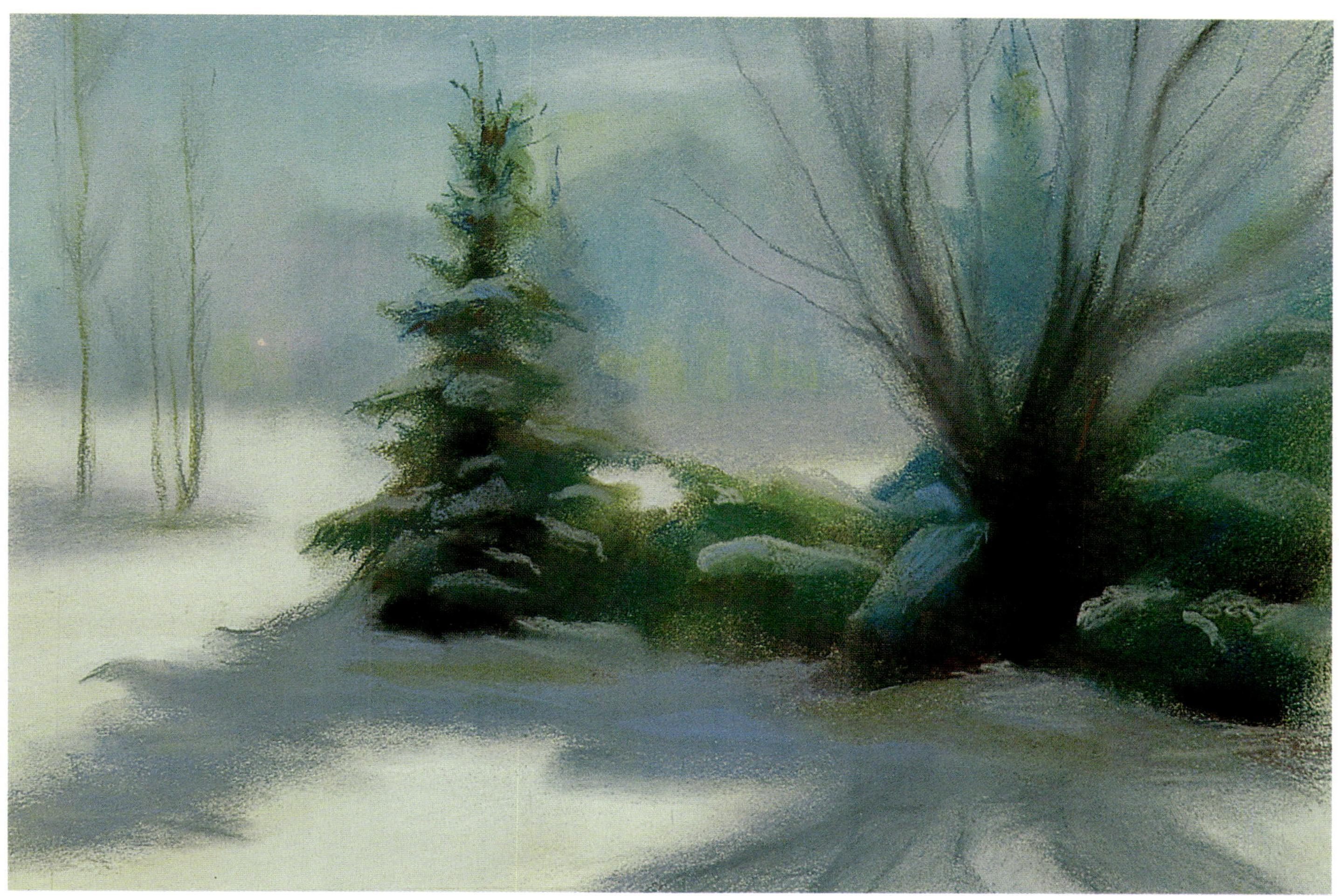

5 Next I render the branches of the pussy willow with mouse gray 3 and burnt sienna 3, keeping the edges soft by blending every stroke. I also add the trunks of the bare trees on the left with mouse gray 5 and raw sienna 5. I draw in the shadowed clumps of snow on the pines with gray 7 and ultramarine blue 7. Because I notice a warm tone in the shadow near the base of the trees, I paint it with olive green 5. Look for changes like this in temperature (not value); these details will strengthen the sense of realism in your paintings.

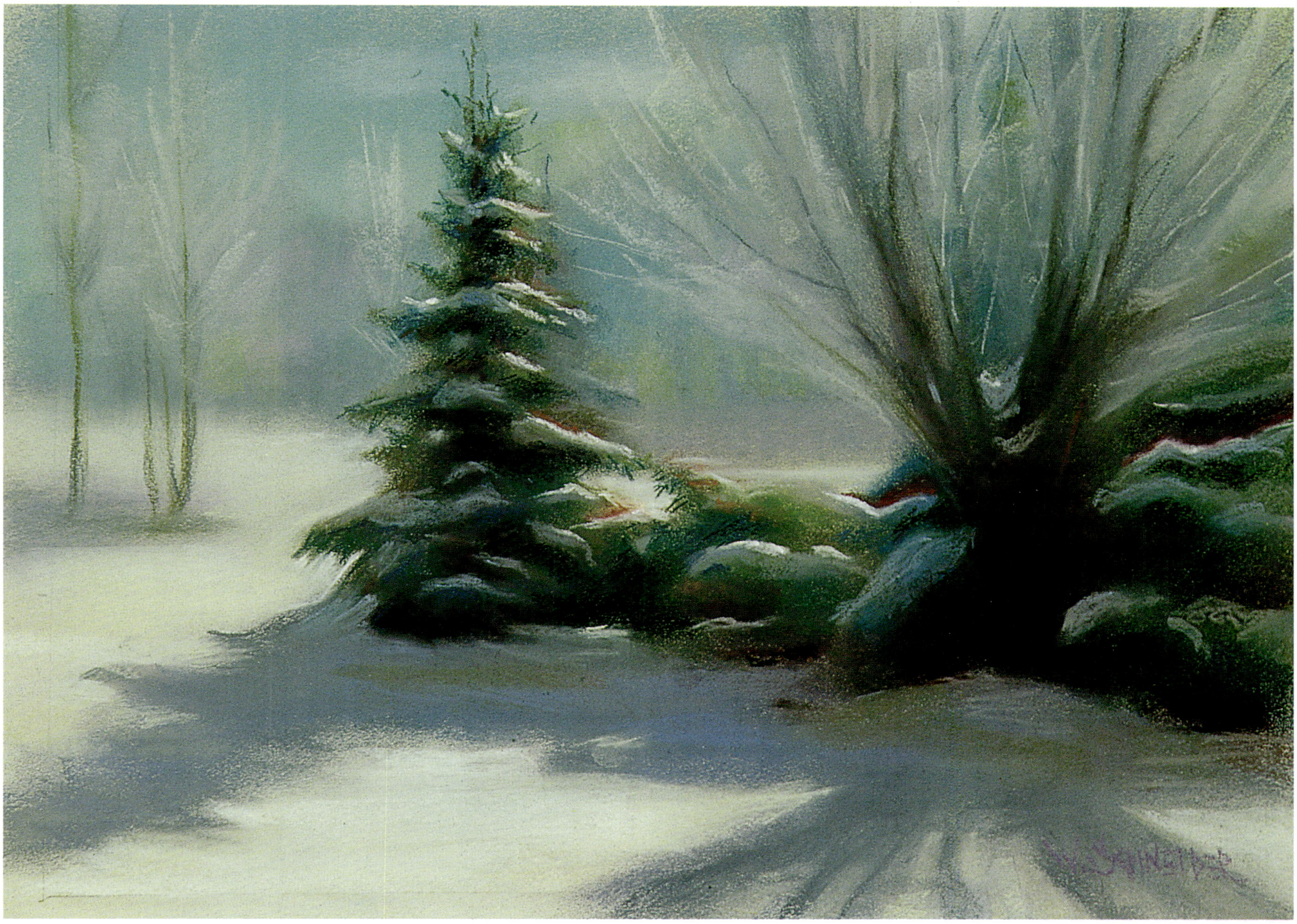

6 Here I add deep yellow 12 and white for the highlights on the snow on the edge of the boughs. I outline the white in some areas with permanent red light 5 and blend it away from the snow. This creates the effect of warmth in the air above the snow. I use green-gray 9 to indicate the frosty, backlit branches of the trees on the left and the pussy willow branches on the right. To sharpen the edge on the left side of the pine, I use deep yellow 12 and leave those strokes unblended. I make sure there is always at least one sharp edge in any subject. If all the edges are equally soft in a painting, the subject can look fuzzy. And if all the edges are hard (a common mistake), then the painting will look as if the objects were flat cutouts pasted onto the background.

Deciding What to Paint

Choosing a subject to paint can be challenging because there are so many fascinating options available. But selecting what to paint is also a wonderful expression of your personal style, taste, and creativity. The more strongly you feel about your subject, the more your emotions will show through in your work, and the more successful your paintings will be. So try to pick something that you care about or that inspires you in your own life—your children, your garden, your favorite pet, last summer's vacation photos, or your own region's natural wonders. For this painting, I was moved by the majesty of Mount Rushmore. The idea of looking up to the founding fathers of our country appeals to me, and I like the composition and sharp perspective of this scene. Looking up from a worm's eye view emphasizes the grandeur of the monument. And for me, the dramatic contrast between the solid, pristine blue sky and the numerous gray colors in the rocks makes this painting that much more inspiring and compelling.

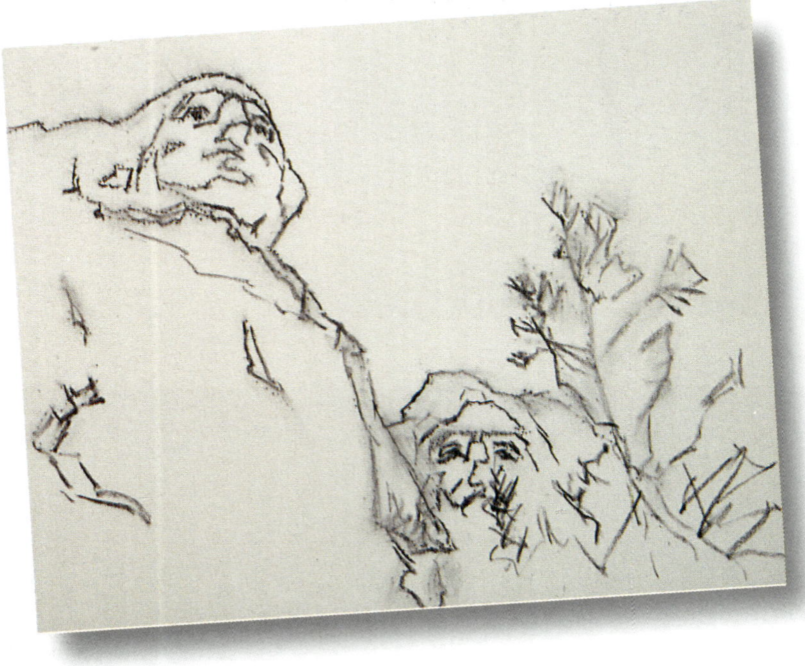

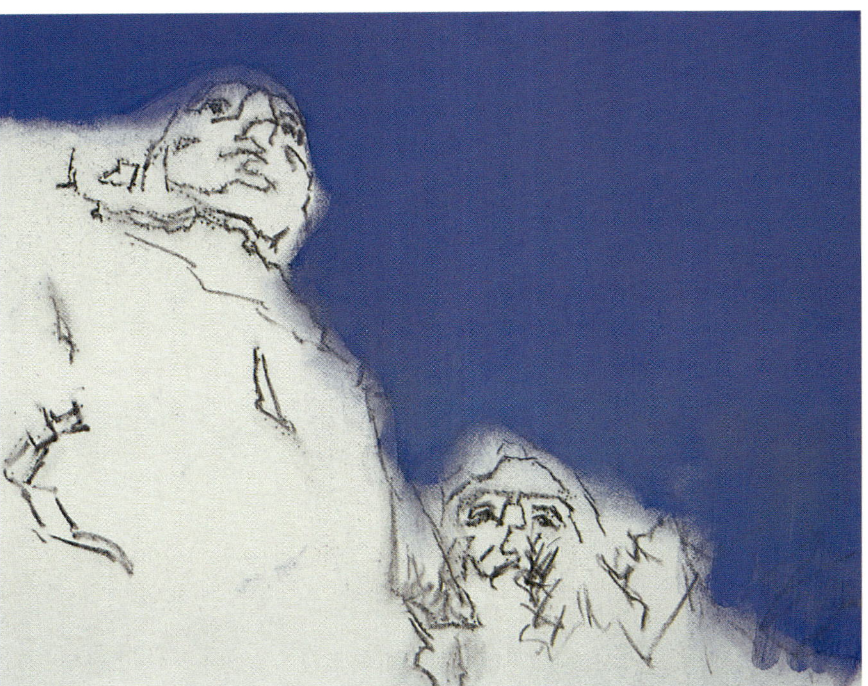

TRANSFERRING A DRAWING Because this drawing needs to be precise and the sanded board I'm using makes it difficult to erase any lines, I first work out the composition on a piece of translucent paper. Next I punch tiny holes in the paper along the lines of the design. Then I place the perforated drawing (called a "cartoon") on top of the pastel board and apply charcoal dust to the outline with a soft brush. The charcoal dust goes through the holes, thus transferring the design to the pastel board. Then I connect the dots on the board with a piece of vine charcoal.

1 I start painting by blocking in the intense blue of the sky. (Notice that I won't be distributing the colors in a equal ratio; more than half of the picture area will be the blue sky.) First I apply a base of sapphire blue 5 and wash it into the tooth of the board with denatured alcohol and a brush. Although the sky seems very even, it is actually composed of a number of colors: I add ultramarine blue 5, cobalt blue 5, lemon yellow 7, and red-violet 7 and blend them well with the side of my hand. Then I place a little more lemon yellow and red-violet at the bottom.

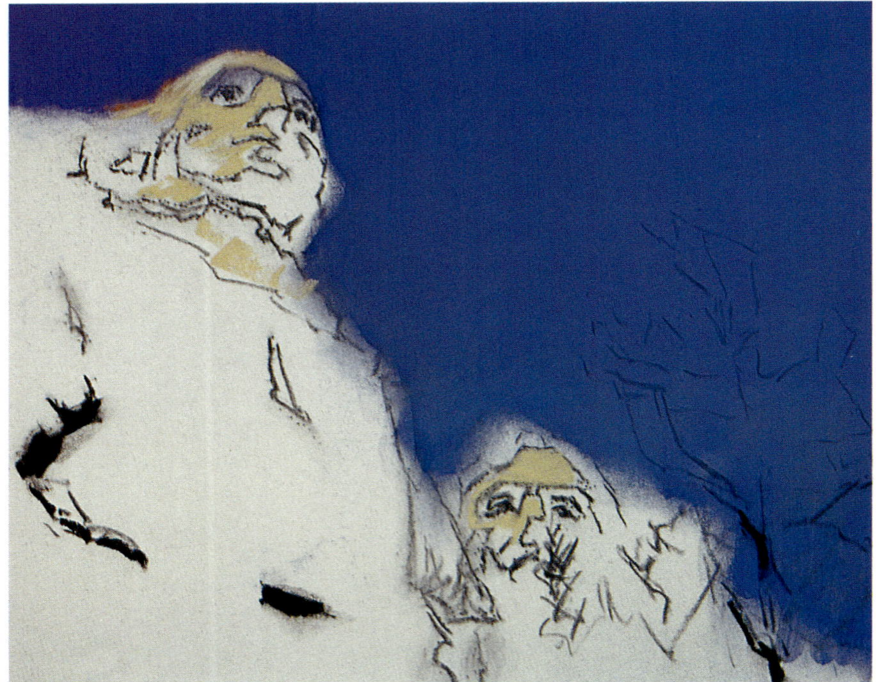

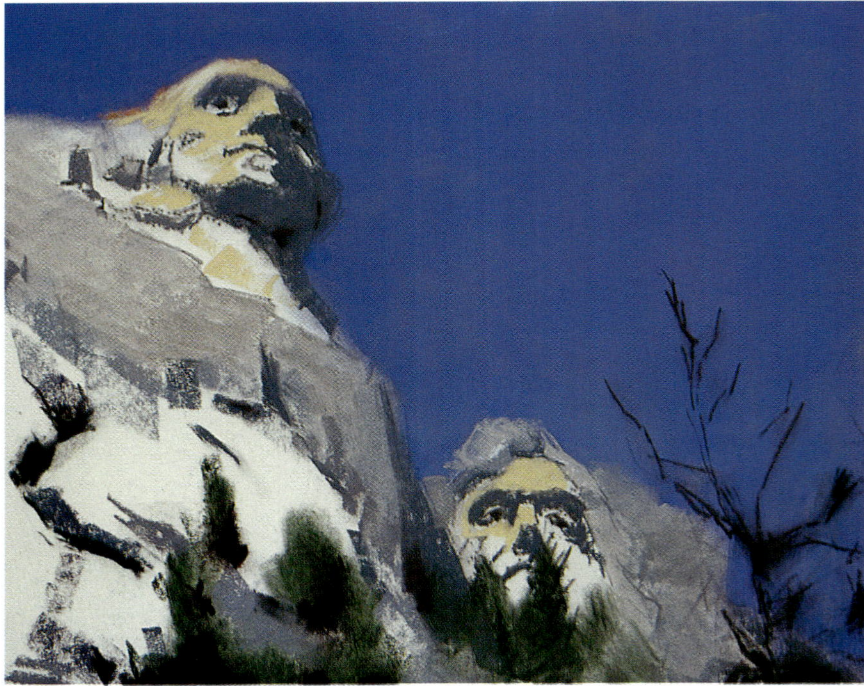

2 Next I paint my darkest dark, bistre 3, in the crevices of the rocks. I am careful to select those crevices that emphasize the perspective; notice that they point toward Washington's head. Then I apply lightest light with yellow ochre 7 and 9, and I add a little permanent red light 5 for a "halo" effect at the top of Washington's head. Next I redraw the tree on the right with charcoal; this tree is important to the design because it helps establish the scale of the massive stone sculpture.

3 Now I paint in the shadow pattern on the mountain with mouse gray 3. The sunlight is warm, so the shadows are cool (they're picking up some of the blue of the sky). Since I'm rendering stone, I blend my strokes much less than I normally would. Harder edges "read" as more angled planes, which is perfect for painting rocks. Then I place the darks in the trees with Mars violet 3, carmine brown 3, and bistre 3. I block in the rest of the trees with blue-green 3, and I apply gray 8 to the roughly chiseled stone below Washington's face.

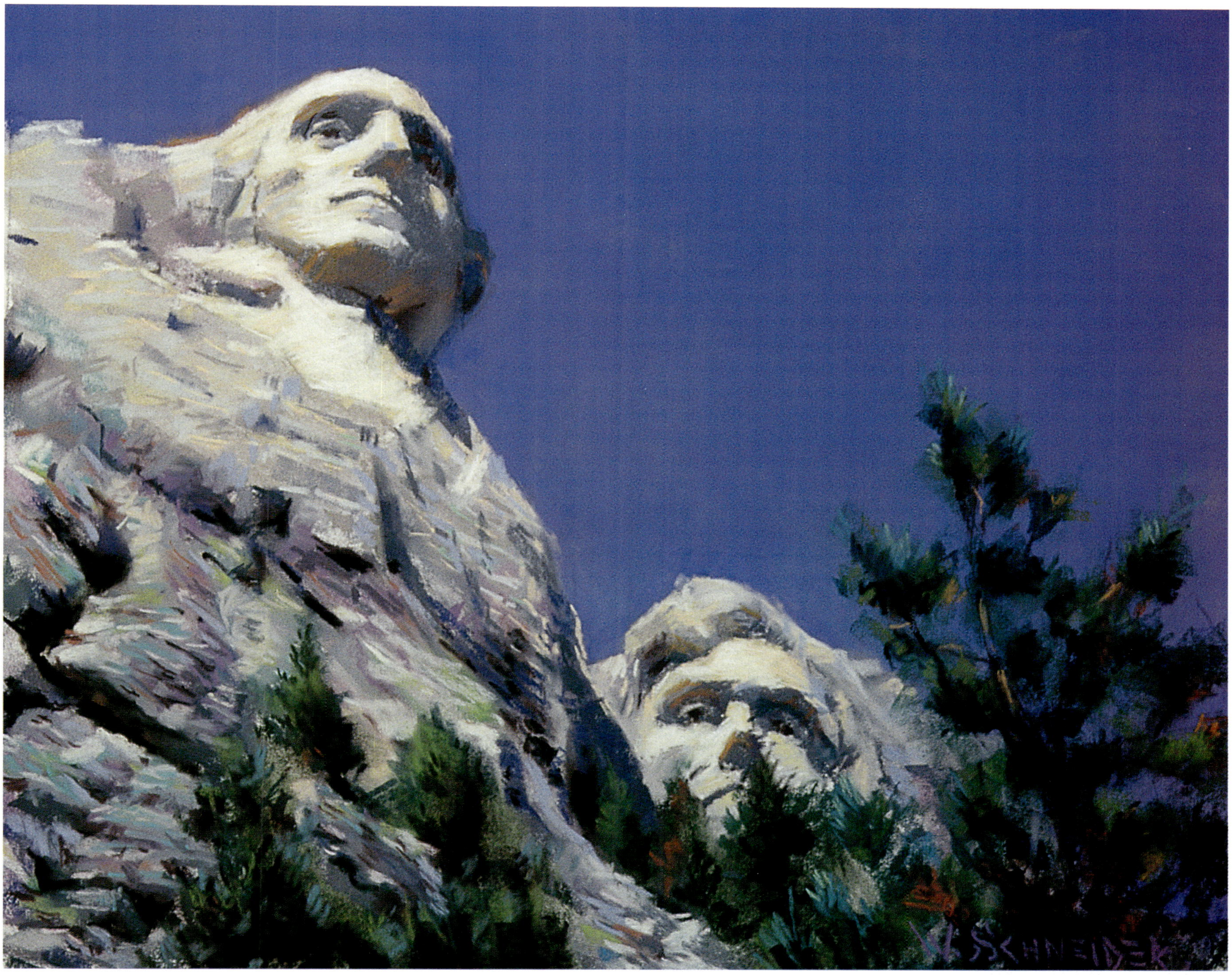

6 To complete the painting, I add the final details. I use black to deepen the crevice on the left side of the painting, and I indicate some of the lighter areas of the pine trees with chrome green 5 and blue-green 7. Then I sharpen some of the sunlit edges on Washington's head with gold ochre 10 and orange 12. Finally I use burnt sienna 5 to render the dead pine needles on a few of the branches. Satisfied with my work, I choose a cool purple hue (Mars violet) that won't stand out too dramatically to sign my name.

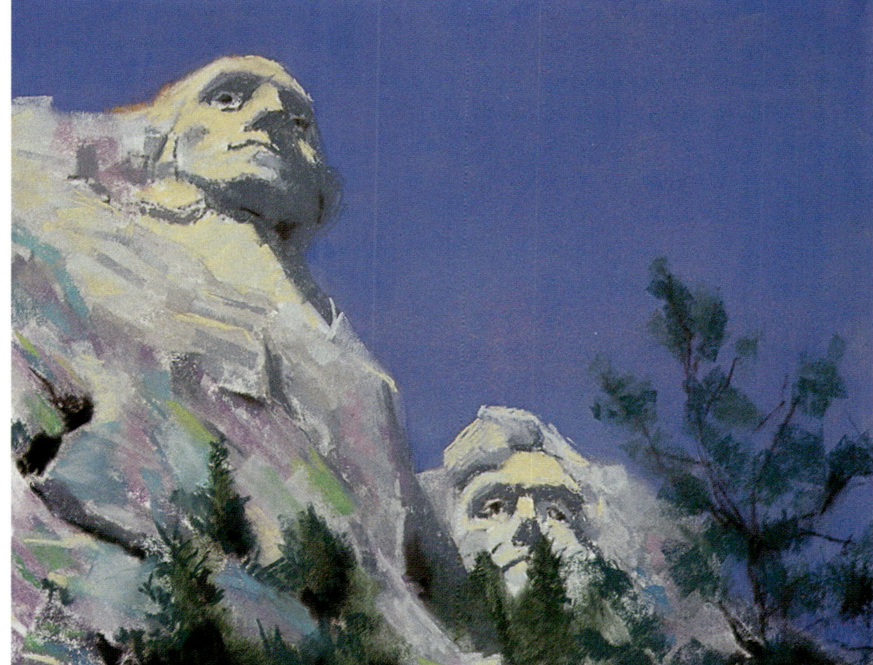

4 Although the tone of the mountain is much less intense than the bright blue sky, it's still very colorful and more than a compilation of various shades of gray. Here I begin by applying strokes of blue-violet 5 and turquoise blue 7 to block in the base colors of the mountain. Then I tone down these hues with green-gray 9 and gray 8. Again, because of the character of the rock, I want to keep harder edges here, so I do not blend these strokes to any great degree. (See page 6 for more on edges.)

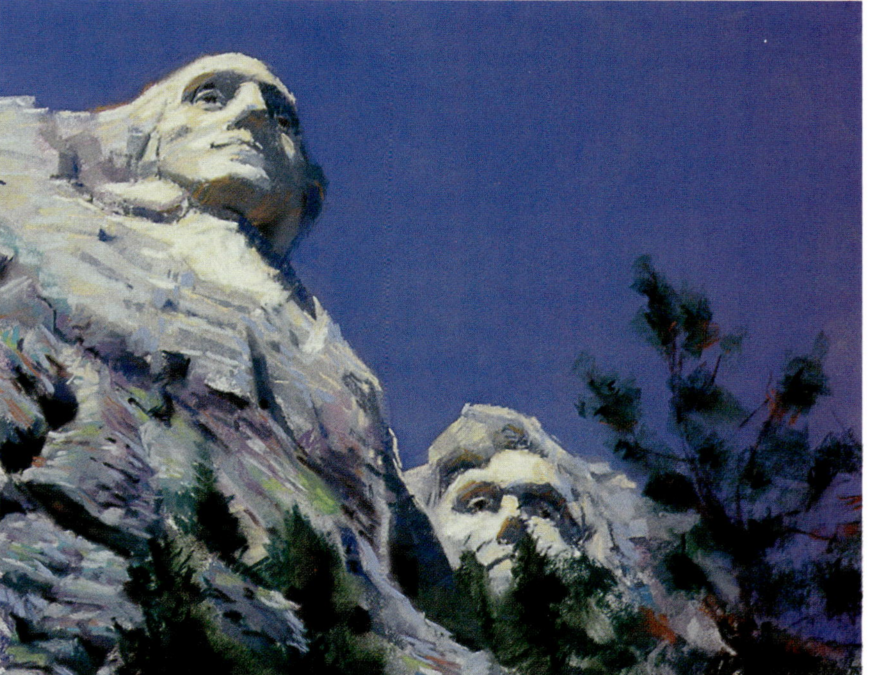

5 Now I begin to add the finishing touches. I deepen some of the key dark areas with carmine brown 3, bistre 3, and black-green 3. The reflected light under Washington's chin and brow is an important detail that helps define the form—I paint it with permanent red light 5, burnt sienna 5, and caput mortuum red 7. Then I modify the green in the rocks with olive green 8 and green-gray 9, and I indicate some of the smaller cracks and recesses with carmine brown 3. Next I lighten the sunlit areas of the heads with yellow ochre 10 and orange 12.

Painting Outdoors

The best thing you can do to hone your artistic skills is to go out-doors and paint directly from life. And because pastel is such a rapid and responsive medium, it is ideal for painting *en plein air* and recording the effects that often change so quickly in nature. Morning dew, shifting clouds, crashing waves—all can be captured with a few quick, decisive strokes. For this painting of a pond near my home, I was able to re-create the cool morning light before the sun warmed the scene and the colors shifted. Another advantage of pastel is that I don't have to premix my pigments, wait for the colors to dry, or worry about keeping brushes clean—in short, there are no tiresome procedures to dampen my spirits or lessen my response to the subject. And because I don't need the extra supplies that some other media require—such as brushes, knives, or mixing mediums— my traveling art pack is light and easy to carry. Then I just lay out my pastels, and I'm ready to start!

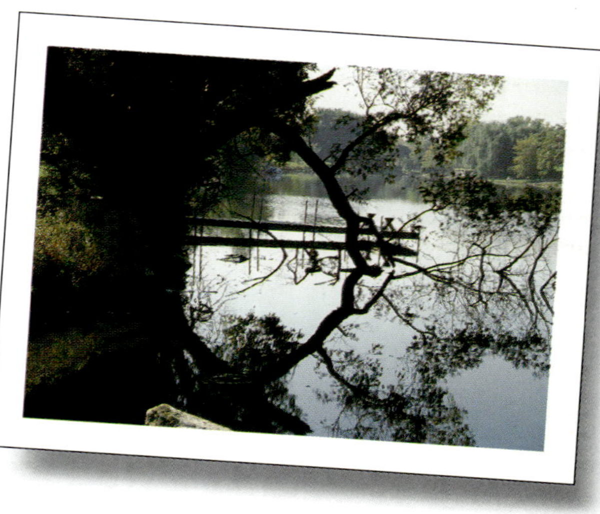

▶ **WORKING FROM LIFE**
Even though it may seem more convenient to paint from photos, they're really only pale imitations of na-ture. Compare this photo to my final painting, and no-tice the nuances of color and value that are lost in the photograph. The two darkest values both be-come black, and the light-est values turn to white. And squinting your eyes while looking at a snap-shot doesn't help you simp-lify the values or see the hardest edges, the way squinting outdoors does.

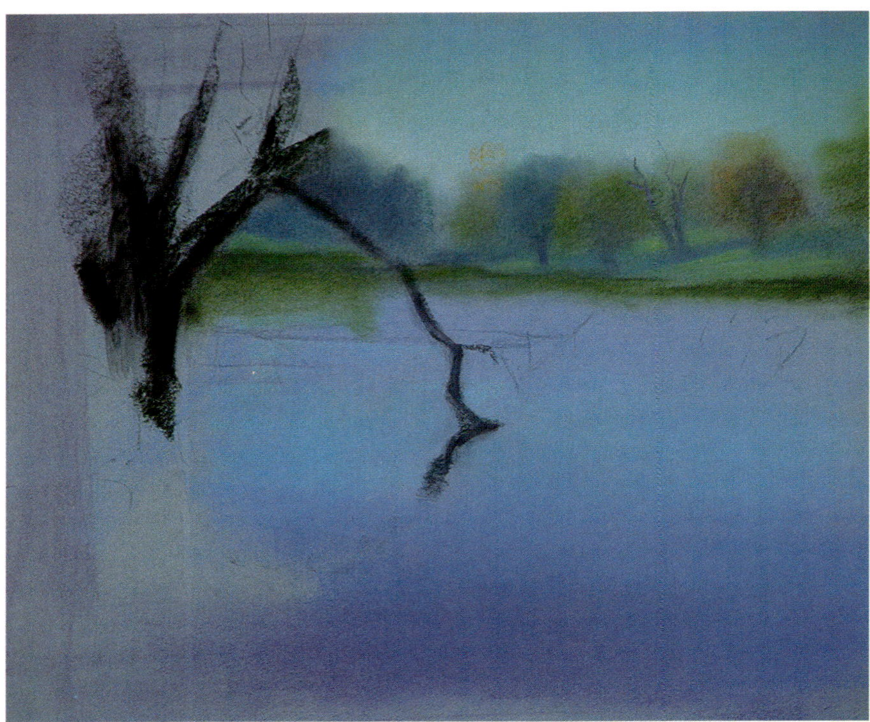

1 I begin by toning the light areas of my light blue paper with thin layers of light yellow 5, red-violet 7, and cobalt blue 5, using the side of my hand to rub the pastel into the tooth of the paper. Then I sketch in the main elements of the scene with vine charcoal and begin painting the black in the tree mass. Next I paint the sky with layers of cobalt blue 5 near the top, turquoise 7 and raw sienna 7 in the middle, and cobalt blue 7 near the bottom. I also add lemon yellow 5 near the horizon, since clear skies tend to be darker at the top and lighter and creamier near the horizon. Then I paint the trees on the far shore with mouse gray 5 for the trunks and the deepest shadows and olive green 5 for the light areas. I gray the trees further with a layer of red-violet 5 to enhance the sense of depth. For variety I add blue-green 5 to a few trees and burnt sienna 5 to another, blending each stroke with the side of my little finger.

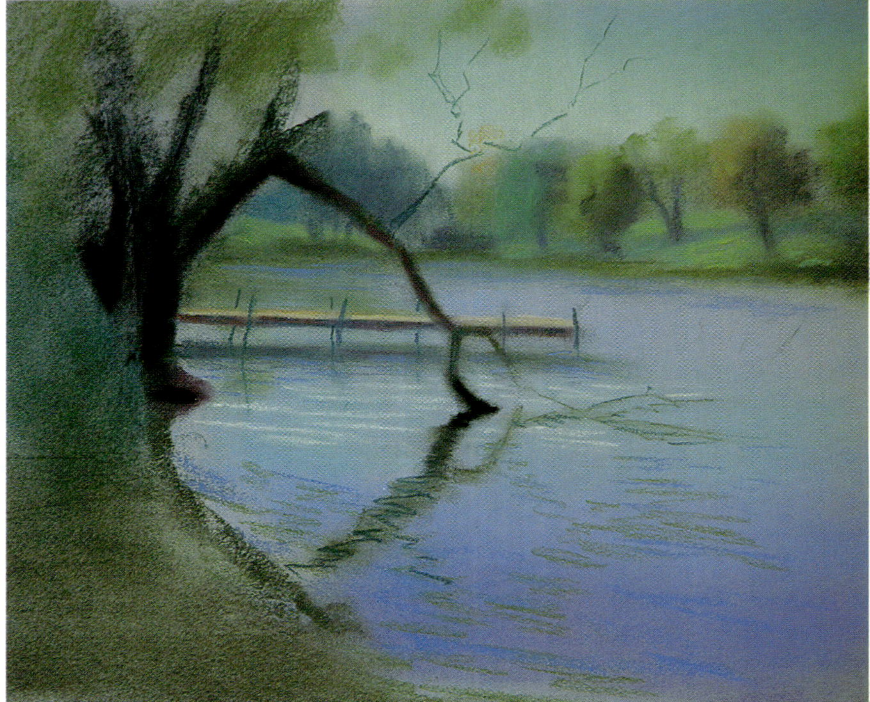

2 Water is like a mirror—it reflects the colors in the sky as well as the colors of nearby ob-jects. Because the darker area of the water is closest and the lightest area is farthest away (reflecting the horizon), I add blue-violet 5 and cobalt blue 5 to the foreground water and red-violet 7 to the background. Then I blend the color transitions in the sky and water with the side of my hand and add a few strokes of lemon yellow 7 for highlights on the water. For the light areas of the dock, I use gold ochre 7, and for the darks I use mouse gray 5 and red-violet deep 3. I block in the general mass of the closest tree using olive green 3. Then I start to add a warmer Indian red 3 to the trunk. I paint dark reflections on the water with olive green 3 and gray-green 3, and I work chrome green 8 grayed with red-violet 8 to the light areas on the far shore to indicate the sunlit grass.

Setups for Painting *en Plein Air*

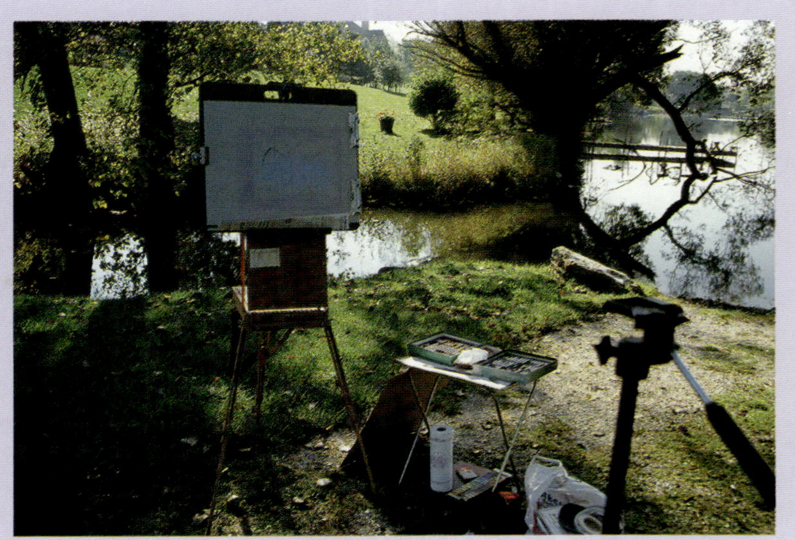

When I paint outdoors, I use a French easel that is light and easy to trans-port. I place my support on a board with clips, and I use a TV tray to hold my pastels (although you can buy portable pastel boxes that attach easily to a portable easel). You may also want to bring a folding chair or collapsi-ble stool if you prefer to sit while painting. I've found it's best to work on smaller supports when plein air painting—they are easier to transport and deal with, and there is less surface space you have to cover in a limited timeframe. Plastic bags are handy for disposing of any trash, and you might consider bringing along some clips or twine to secure your setup in case it gets windy. Sunscreen and/or a hat are essential (even on cloudy days), and you should never hike out too far without some food and water. The more flexible you can be when you're painting outdoors, the more you will enjoy the experience. Nature provides an endless array of subject matter—so go outdoors and have fun painting in pastel!

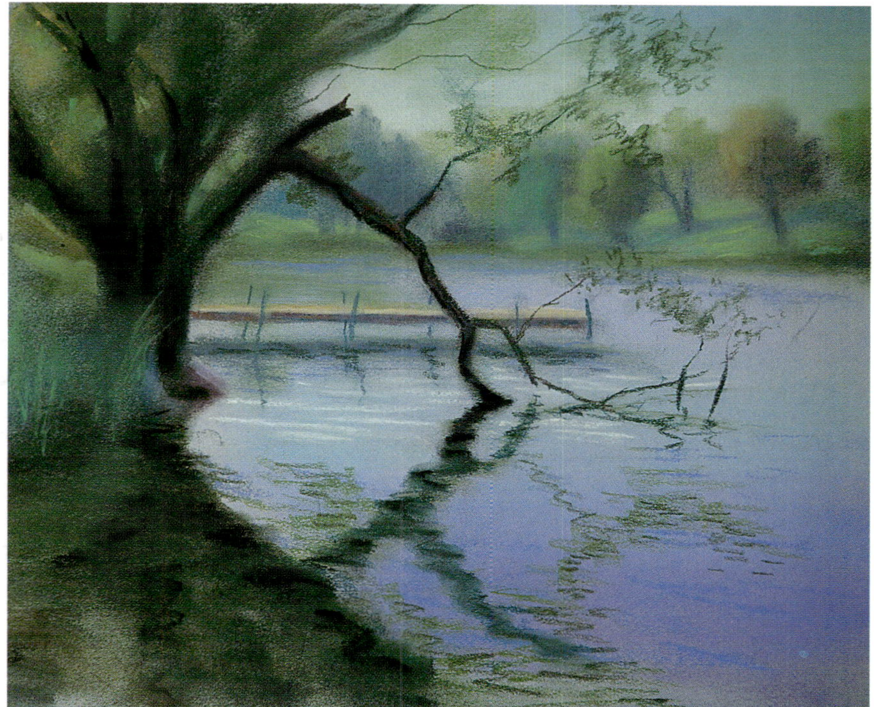 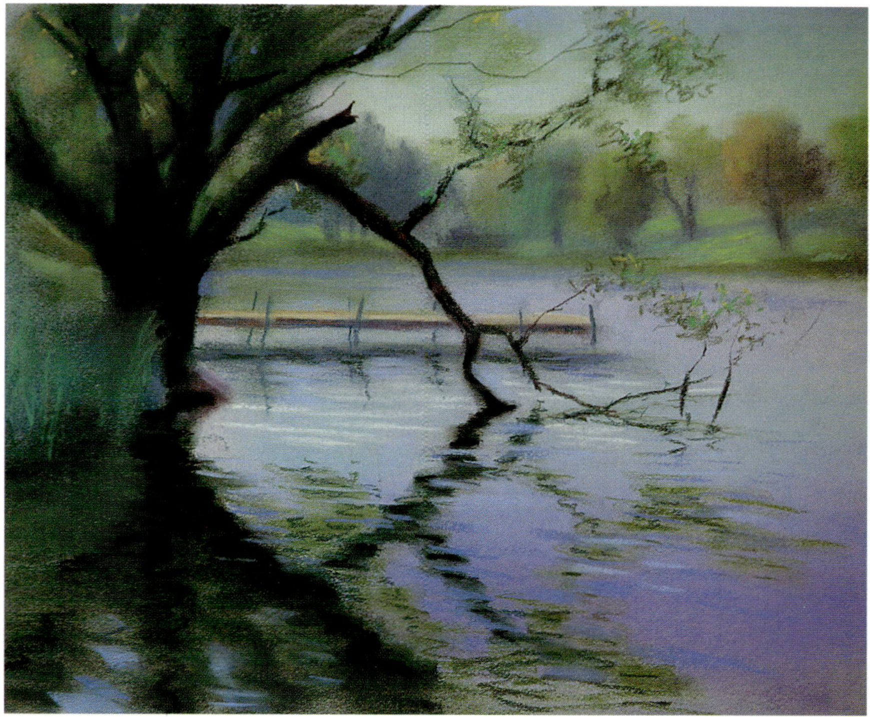

3 Because water is an imperfect mirror, the reflections are darker than the objects reflected (but very dark objects appear slightly lighter in reflections). Here I darken the tree mass and the reflection with gray-green 3 and burnt sienna 3. Then I sharpen the edges of the broken branch by painting some of the sky color into its edges. Next I add leaves with olive green 3 and define the spaces between the branches with strokes of olive green 8 and orange 5. Then I use a few strokes of olive green 5 to indicate the grass near the tree trunk.

4 Next I add strokes of ultramarine blue 5 in the water to represent the sky holes in the reflection of the tree. Here I blend my strokes less than elsewhere so they appear bolder. Then I apply cobalt blue 5 to indicate ripples cutting across the reflected branches. Next I add a few more warm darks to the trees with burnt sienna 3. Then I add a hint of the sky color behind the tree with cobalt blue 5 and blend it into some of the spaces between branches (the negative spaces).

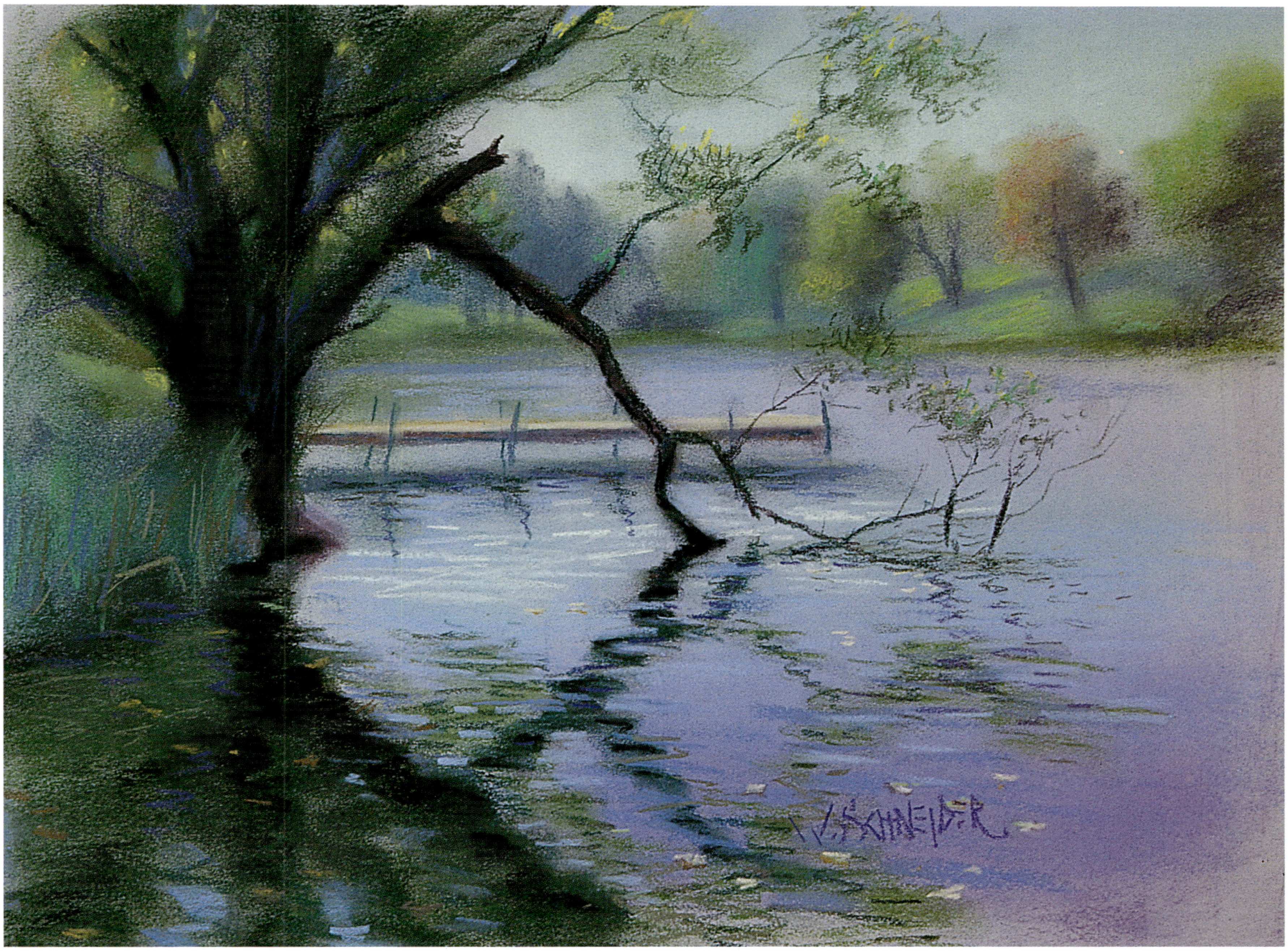

5 To make water appear flat, it helps to somehow indicate its surface plane—the definition of the edge of the shore, the highlights, the ripples, and any floating surface matter can all help to create that illusion. Here I add more highlights to the water with deep yellow 9 and place a few of the floating leaves on the surface of the water. I use yellow ochre 3 on the shadowed sides of the floating leaves and gold ochre 5 in the light areas. Then I draw a thin, dark shadow with Indian red 3 below some of the leaves to deepen the cast shadows. As a finishing touch, I add strokes of orange 5 in the foreground tree to indicate some backlit leaves. Finally I place a few strokes of gold ochre 3 to deepen the green grasses near the trunk, and my piece is complete.

Walter Foster Art Instruction Program

THREE EASY STEPS TO LEARNING ART

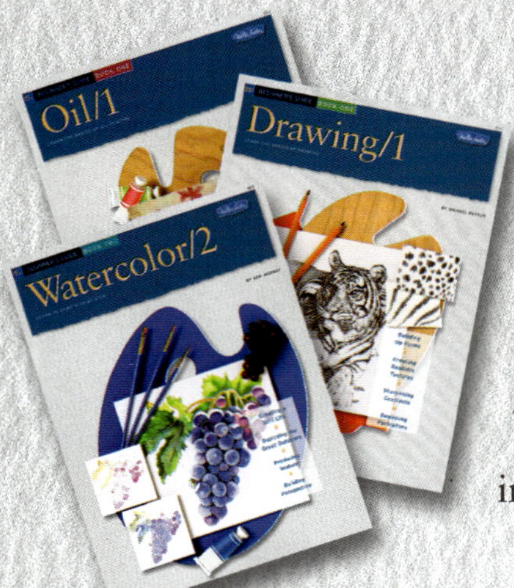

Beginner's Guides are specially written to encourage and motivate aspiring artists. This series introduces the various painting and drawing media—acrylic, oil, pastel, pencil, and watercolor—making it the perfect starting point for beginners. Book One introduces the medium, showing some of its diverse possibilities through beautiful rendered examples and simple explanations, and Book Two instructs with a set of engaging art lessons that follow an easy step-by-step approach.

How to Draw and Paint titles contain progressive visual demonstrations, expert advice, and simple written explanations that assist novice artists through the next stages of learning. In this series, professional artists tap into their experience to walk the reader through the artistic process step by step, from preparation work and preliminary sketches to special techniques and final details. Organized by medium, these books provide insight into an array of subjects.

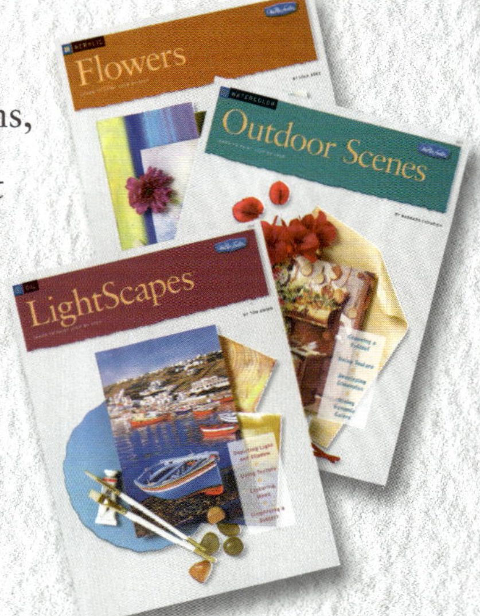

Artist's Library titles offer both beginning and advanced artists the opportunity to expand their creativity, conquer technical obstacles, and explore new media. Written and illustrated by professional artists, the books in this series are ideal for anyone aspiring to reach a new level of expertise. They'll serve as useful tools that artists of all skill levels can refer to again and again.

Walter Foster products are available at art and craft stores everywhere.
Write or call for a FREE catalog that includes all of Walter Foster's titles,
or visit our website at www.walterfoster.com.

WALTER FOSTER PUBLISHING, INC.
23062 La Cadena Drive
Laguna Hills, California 92653
Main Line 949/380-7510
Toll Free 800/426-0099

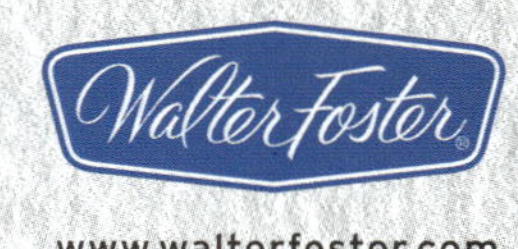

www.walterfoster.com